A Fish Feast

by Charlotte Wright

Pacific Search Press

To my family
Chatt, Brook, Jon, and Shelley

Pacific Search Press, 222 Dexter Avenue North,
    Seattle, Washington 98109
©1982 by Charlotte Wright. All rights reserved
Printed in the United States of America

Edited by Marlene Leamon
Designed by Judy Petry
Illustrated by Mike Foster

Library of Congress Cataloging in Publication Data

Wright, Charlotte.
    A fish feast.

    Includes index.
    1. Cookery (Fish)   I. Title.
TX747.W74   1982   641.6'92   82-14157
ISBN 0-914718-73-8

Contents

Acknowledgments 7
Introduction 9
   My Favorite Fish 10
   How to Select a Fresh Fish 11
   Special Ingredients 14
Steamed, Poached, and Baked 26
Sautéed and Fried 57
Broiled and Barbecued 77
Favorite Specialties 87
Gumbo and Chowder 101
Crepes, Appetizers, and Hors d'Oeuvres 108
Sauces 129
Entertaining with Flair 143
   The Setting 144
   The Wines 146
U.S. and Metric Measurements 192
Index 195

Acknowledgments

First, I wish to thank Walter and Cyrus Tamashiro of Tamashiro Market for graciously permitting me to talk at length with Larry Konishi, and second, I wish to thank Guy Tamashiro for answering my questions when Larry wasn't there. Foremost, I want to thank Larry Konishi for his genuine manner and patience. His detailed knowledge of the fish in the Hawaiian waters guided me in experimenting with different fish and in learning about their subtleties.

On the West Coast, I wish to thank Jamie Tadique from Pike Place Fish Company in Seattle for his ability to deliver a wealth of informative, important details in a short period of time.

In addition, I am most grateful to my friends. The following people, listed alphabetically, contributed personal recipes which have been included: Kris Allison, Olive Brown, Shirley Burt, Judy Capellino, Joan Chang, Leslie Connolly, Jim Dittmar, Marion Gedeon, Connie Hereford, Jean Hindman, Charles Izumoto, Jr., Michel Martin, Caroline Oda, Tom Reaves, Jeanne Reinhart, Enid Wade, Charmaine Weinberg, Camille and Jack Wilson, Louise Wright, and Gwen and Sheldon Zane. Similarly, other friends contributed pivotal ideas which led to the birth of other recipes: Bill Adams, Louis Capellino, Roy Carpenter, Risé Dittmar, Donna Hicks, Kay Tierney, and Wilma Wilkie.

Finally, a special thanks to Walter Takeda for his illustrations of how to clean squid, to Mike Foster for his original sketches and even more importantly, for his time and good wishes, to Richard Dean for his time and selection of wines, to Francis Oda for his creative suggestion of title, and to Marlene Leamon for her patient and considerate editing.

To all of you and others unnamed, *mahalo!*

Introduction

My mother often said, "Charlotte, find a good man and stick with him." I view cooking from a similar perspective—find good recipes and stick with them. For me, a good recipe is a personal combination of taste, budget, appearance (or entertainment value), and convenience in preparation.

This book contains my favorite recipes for cooking fish. Generally, I like fish without many bones that are light and delicate in taste and that are somewhat firm in texture. In fact, I enjoy fish so much and find it so simple to prepare that a fish dish has become my trademark in entertaining. When one of my guests took a photograph of one of my fish entrées, I decided to write this book. Fortunately, most of the recipes are easy to prepare. Fortunately, too, fish, with its compact weight, limited calories, and high nutritive value, is an excellent buy.

While some recipes for shellfish are included, I have deliberately kept the focus of the book on fish. There are hundreds of recipes available for shellfish, and most are expensive. Observations and conversations have convinced me that the daily chef has a limited repertoire for cooking fish, yet would like to know more if the process could be painless and relatively simple.

For most recipes, at least two kinds of fish are suggested—one from the Pacific-Atlantic waters and one from the Hawaiian waters. However, substitutions are feasible. Even freshwater fish can be substituted for saltwater fish, provided the fat content of the fish is similar. The fat content is the most important factor in interchanging recipes.

If a recipe may benefit from the use of a commercial convenience product, I suggest it. In addition, some recipes are specifically designed for microwave use, and others can be readily converted.

Finally, when I entertain, I want an appealing meal which can be prepared in advance so that I'm able to enjoy my guests. If a recipe calls for extraordinary kitchen work after my guests have arrived, forget it. I complete any extraordinary assembling the day before or the day of the party.

In the section "Entertaining with Flair" are menus for formal dinners, informal dinners, brunches, and luncheons. While the entrée in each is a recipe from an earlier section, suggestions and recipes appear for the remaining courses, along with instructions for preparation and presentation.

A final afterthought: too often entertaining is reserved for company only. However, one of my romantic fantasies centers around entertaining for my mate. The setting is a sleek, sophisticated penthouse which commands sweeping views of the city. A formal table for two is set on the veranda with the sparkling city lights as a backdrop. The last touch of azure blue is fading on the horizon. Tapered white candles are lit, potted azaleas are blooming, and a lovely nosegay centerpiece is placed perfectly on a white linen cloth. Dressed in an extravagant peignoir and gown, I cross the plush carpeting of the chic apartment. The seductive perfume lingers in the air. A gentle, romantic breeze ushers me through the opened, sliding doorway to the veranda, and my peignoir billows behind me, creating a floating effect. Nothing heavy for dinner this night; there is a small kumu (Hawaiian fish) steaming in the oven.

It might be fun to try on that fantasy suburban-style. Plan for a full moon. Farm out the children. Arrange the candles and wine glasses, and yes, do buy a small nosegay because it makes *you* feel special. Slip into something comfortable and play your favorite soft jazz or mood music. And of course, for a divine, but light dinner, have a moist, succulent fish steaming in the oven, such as the Oven-Steamed Kumu with Capers and Wine. After all, Aphrodite, goddess of love, was created from the foam of the sea.

My Favorite Fish

When I moved from the Pacific Coast to Hawaii, I left a cooking experience of salmon and trout for the unknown qualities of mahimahi and opakapaka. I couldn't even pronounce the names, much less prepare them. Many times I longed for a simple guide which would name a few key fish and tell a little about them without overwhelming my occupied-elsewhere mind. On the next several pages are my own efforts to create two such simple lists, one for my favorite fish in the Pacific-Atlantic waters and one for my favorite Hawaiian fish.

Since fish are usually classed for cooking purposes by fat content and because this information about fat content is helpful in determining what fish are interchangeable in recipes, I've provided a special chart indicating whether a fish is lean, moist to medium, or oily in nature. In general, fish with a higher fat content, such as steelhead, members of the tuna family, and some salmon, lend themselves to broiling or barbecuing, while other fish with a lower fat content, such as swordfish and halibut, require basting with an oil-based marinade if being broiled or barbecued.

I have learned that opinions, even among the "experts," vary on the oil content of fish, particularly those in the moist to medium category.

Individual taste and the method of cooking seem to play heavily in a decision about the fat content of a fish. The important point is that any fish, regardless of its natural oils, will be dry if overcooked. Therefore, a good rule of thumb is to undercook, rather than overcook, a fish. You can always cook it a few minutes longer.

How to Select a Fresh Fish

Ben Franklin once said that houseguests are like fish; after three days they begin to smell. Now this is not to say that houseguests are unwanted, but rather that fish should be cooked promptly. When I buy fresh fish, I usually cook it within twenty-four hours, forty-eight at the maximum. Therefore, coordinate your trip to the fish market with your cooking plans.

I give five tests when I select a fresh fish, and here they are in the order I give them. If you lack confidence in selecting a fresh fish, then write the test phrases on a notepad and take it with you to the market until you have the procedures down pat.

1. **The "eyeball-to-eyeball" test.** Look for clear, bulging eyes. The fresher the fish, the clearer, shinier, and brighter the eyes. If the fish is aging, the eyes become sunken and increasingly cloudy. If a fish doesn't pass my eyeball-to-eyeball test, I don't even examine it for the second test.

2. **The "redder-the-better" test.** Open the gills of the fish to examine for color and smell. (If you pick up the fish, please do so gently.) The gills are the organs whereby a fish receives oxygen from the water and are located on each side of the fish just behind the jawline, if a fish has a jawline. Fresh gills are a nice reddish color and have a clean smell. When a fish begins to deteriorate, the gills are the first parts to go. They change from a reddish color to a dark brown or a gray and begin giving off a foul, "fishy" odor. Therefore, checking for a good red color and a clean smell is an excellent gauge of the freshness of the fish. Nevertheless, I usually go on to the third test.

3. **The "elastic-is-fantastic" test.** Gently press the body of the fish. The flesh should be firm and any finger imprint should vanish. Of course, if you poke hard, you may damage not only the fish, but your relations with the fishmonger, too. Nevertheless, the message is the same as Madison Avenue's: an elastic, firm flesh is definitely desirable. After this test, I usually know whether I'm interested in the fish or not. If there is any doubt, I continue.

4. **The "play-the-scales" test.** While this is not a musical comedy, take your finger and lightly and quickly run it against the lay of the scales. The scales should remain firmly attached to the body. In addition, the film covering the skin should be clear, not cloudy. Now, if there is any suspicion left, go on to the final test.

5. **The "smell-the-belly" test.** For a final opinion, check the color of the vent; it should be pink, not brown. Take a deep whiff; there should be no offensive, "fishy" odor. Smell the gills again to verify your judgment . . . and of course, you always can ask when the fish was caught.

Of course, it is senseless to select a fish suitable for four people when you're serving twelve. Following is a general guide to help you select the proper amount. Using these amounts, I've never had leftovers except for the sweet meat in the cheeks. So if you are entertaining guests known for their ravenous appetites, please use the higher allowances per person. Normally, I've found that the appetites of guests tend to balance one another; while one eats for two, another eats like the proverbial bird. Nevertheless, it is a good practice to consider the people you are serving before you purchase your fish. Naturally, you will want to consider also the dish you're preparing. Obviously a casserole serving eight requires less fish than a dinner of individual steaks or fillets for eight.

If you have any doubts, ask the fishmonger to help you find the right amount for the people you are serving.

How Much to Buy

Kind of Fish	Portion Size	Amounts Needed
Whole, *uncleaned* fish, including head, skin, and bones. (Remember, the fish is cleaned after it is weighed.)	Allow ⅔ to ¾ pounds per person	Dinner for 4 = 3 pounds Dinner for 6 = 4½ pounds Dinner for 8 = 5¾ pounds Dinner for 10 = 7 pounds Dinner for 12 = 8 pounds
Dressed fish (drawn, scaled with head and tail removed)	Allow ½ pound per person	Dinner for 4 = 2 pounds Dinner for 6 = 3 pounds Dinner for 8 = 4 pounds Dinner for 10 = 5 pounds Dinner for 12 = 6 pounds
Fish steaks or fillets	Allow ¼ to ⅓ pound per person	Dinner for 4 = 1⅓ pounds Dinner for 6 = 1½ to 2 pounds Dinner for 8 = 2 to 2⅔ pounds Dinner for 10 = 2½ to 3⅓ pounds Dinner for 12 = 3 to 4 pounds
Drawn and scaled small fish, such as rainbow trout	Allow 1 fish per person	*Helpful Note:* ¾ pound of boneless fillet yields 1¾ cups of fish.

Special Ingredients

Occasionally an ingredient might be suggested with which you're unfamiliar. If so, I hope it is on this list which, while not comprehensive, attempts to cover the more unusual items and where they may be found.

Anchovy Paste: Small tubes are available in the gourmet section.

Bamboo Shoots: The shoot of the bamboo plant. It is commonly found in cans in the Oriental section of the market. Cut the larger shoots into sections before slicing.

Bamboo Skewers: While these are not ingredients, they are mentioned several times as handy things to have around. They may be found in small packages in the housewares section or in the paper goods area of your grocery. Ideal for barbecuing smaller foods.

Bean Threads (Japanese):   Long, narrow, whitish threads that appear almost plastic. In Hawaii they're also known as long rice. Before using, they are steeped in hot water until pliable. They are located in the Oriental section of the market or an Oriental grocery.

Capers: The greenish flower buds of the caper plant, a small shrub in the Mediterranean region. The buds are pickled and may be found in 3-ounce jars in the gourmet section or near the pickles or chili peppers in the market.

Celeriac Root: Also known as root celery or celery root. It is located with other fresh root vegetables in the market.

Chinese Parsley: Derived from the coriander spice plant, this differs from regular parsley. It's also known as *cilantro.* If available, it will be with other fresh parsleys.

Chinese Pea Pods: Also known as sugar or snow pea pods. They are available fresh or in frozen packages. If fresh, remove the coarse string from the larger ones as you would with fresh green beans.

Chinese Mustard: A hot mustard, available with other bottled mustards in the market or in the gourmet section. It is frequently mixed with soy sauce for dipping wun tun or other foods.

Chorizo: A spicy, Mexican sausage, similar to Polish sausage or Portuguese sausage, but hotter in taste.

Chung Choi (Chinese): A small, dried turnip ball wrapped with some of the green top. It tastes like a white radish. Rinse before chopping. It may be found in the Oriental section of the market or in a Chinese grocery. It is used in soups and often sprinkled as a garnish.

Coconut Milk: Pure coconut milk may be found in cans in the frozen food section near the juices.

Daikon: The Japanese name for the white turnip or giant white radish. It's crisp and excellent eaten raw. It's the traditional bed for sashimi (raw fish). Thin slices are soaked in ice water until they curl, then shredded.

Dashi-no-moto (Japanese): Dashi is a broth made from dried bonito flakes. Dashi-no-moto is a packaged, ready-to-brew soup stock which may be located in the Oriental section of the market or in a Japanese grocery. The soup stock comes in tea bag form or small aluminum packets containing a crushed bouillon mixture. However, since the word "bag" seems to be printed on all of the boxes, even those with packets, you may be uncertain of what you're getting unless you check the contents. Personally I prefer the packets. If you use the bag, do not squeeze it over the soup, for it will result in cloudiness of the broth. Since there are other soup stocks, do double-check the name "dashi-no-moto."

Escoffier Diable Sauce: A pleasant sauce with a mild flavor. It is delicious for basting and may be found in 6-ounce bottles in the gourmet section.

Filé Powder: Also known as Gumbo Filé. It is made of the powdered young leaves of sassafras and is used to thicken soups or stews. It is available in small jars in the gourmet section.

Ito-wakame (Japanese): A dried, brownish-green seaweed available in the Oriental section or in an Oriental grocery. Health food stores also carry dried seaweed of many varieties. Soak in warm water until pliable.

Kielbasa: A Polish sausage which is commonly available in the refrigerated section housing cold cuts, bacon, and spreads.

Kombu (Japanese): A dried tangle seaweed, deep olive-green in color. It should be soaked in water until pliable before using.

Mandarin Oranges: A canned variety, similar in taste to a tangerine. It may be found in the canned fruit section or the Oriental or possibly gourmet sections. If unavailable, substitute canned apricot halves.

Mirin (Japanese):   A sweet rice wine often labeled as "sweet cooking sauce," "sweet cooking rice wine," or "cooking mirin." It's often located with the soy sauce or vinegars; otherwise, a Japanese grocery will stock it and perhaps a larger liquor store. Sake or cooking sherry make suitable substitutes.

Panko (Japanese):   A crispy flour meal used in breading that is available in the Oriental section of the market or in a Japanese grocery. In Hawaii two common brands are Mum's and Marukai. I prefer Mum's because it offers the panko in "fine" and in "flakes," and I prefer the fine texture. (Mum's is handled by Taisei Trading Co., Ltd., Kobe, Japan 657.)

Pickapeppa Sauce: A tangy sauce somewhat similar in taste to chutney. Of Jamaican origin, it is composed of tomatoes, onions, mangoes, raisins, tamarinds, and yummy spices.

Portuguese Vinha D'alhos: An excellent marinade for fish. It may be made from scratch or purchased as a packaged dry mix from NOH Foods International, P.O. Box 8392, Honolulu, Hawaii 96815. (Very inexpensive, I might add, and worth obtaining.) When opening the dry mix, do turn your head, before the fine, hot powder enters the nostrils.

Rock Salt: Coarse crystals of sea salt, also called Hawaiian rock salt in Hawaii. Sea salt is readily available in the salt section, and is usually rubbed into fish or meat.

Sake (Japanese):   The Japanese version of wine, sake is a white rice wine and is always served warmed. It is available in liquor stores, Oriental markets, or gourmet outlets. There are even sake sets that are comprised of a small server which looks something like a short bud vase with a big bottom and six tiny sake cups. To heat the sake, pour into the server and place the server in a pan filled with two inches of water. Heat over medium temperature until sake is warmed. This is pronounced sä-ké.

Sesame Oil: A fine oil with a nutty flavor. It's sold in a regular market, possibly the Oriental section, but health food stores also carry it.

Teriyaki (Japanese):   A Japanese barbecue sauce. It is readily available in packages of dry mix or bottled in the market. It also may be ordered from NOH Foods International, P.O. Box 8392, Honolulu, Hawaii 96815. (A parenthetical note here is in order. This firm also carries a packaged dry mix called Korean Pul-ko-gee which is the most superb marinade sauce for steaks I've ever had, and it's so easy.)

Ti Leaves: Large, smooth green leaves from the ti plant in Hawaii or other subtropical areas. Leaves are used as cooking wrappers much like parchment paper. They are also used as a bed for presenting foods, and strung together, they form the authentic Hawaiian hula skirt. They also decorate large stages and platforms, and in legend their growth helped ward off evil spirits from the home.

Tofu: Bean cake made from the milky liquid pressed out of the soybean. It is of custard-like consistency and shaped in a block which slices or cubes easily. High in nutriments, particularly protein, it is found in the refrigerated section of the market. Once purchased, it should be used within several days. Drain before using.

Wasabi (Japanese):   A hot green horseradish powder, it is mixed with water to form a paste and served with soy sauce for sashimi (raw fish). It comes in a small can and may be found in the Oriental section of the market or in a Japanese grocery.

Water Chestnuts: These canned nuts are readily available in most markets. If fresh, they should be pared, then sliced and used as if canned.

Wun Tun Pi (Chinese):   Also commonly referred to as won ton noodles or won ton pi. These are thin, 3-inch square wrappers made of pastry. They may be found in the refrigerated section, in the frozen food section of the market, or in a Chinese grocery.

Pacific-Atlantic Fish

Fish	Fat Content		
	lean	moist to medium	oily
Bluefish	x		
Codfish	x		
Flounder* or Sole		x	
Haddock (Scrod)	x		
Halibut	x		
Herring		x	
Mackerel			x
Mullet		x	
Pompano		x	
Porgy		x	
Pacific Snapper		x	
Red Snapper		x	
Rockfish			
Black Cod (Butterfish)		x	
Lingcod	x		
Rock Cod	x		
Sea Trout		x	
Yellow Rockfish		x	

* Turbot, a member of the flounder family, is imported from Greenland and is usually frozen. However, occasionally fish markets will carry it fresh.

Comments
The large sole which is so tasty is called petrale.
Many say this tastes like chicken.
In the Northwest, the authentic red snapper is called the Pacific snapper.
The fillets sold as red snapper are usually yellow rockfish.
Black cod is also known as butterfish and is especially good in casseroles.
Fine eating fish; may come in shades of green or yellow.
This has a slightly different flavor from other rockfish; Oriental cuisine usually steams it or makes soup with it.
Usually sold as red snapper fillets in the Northwest; very tasty.

Pacific-Atlantic Fish, continued

Fish	Fat Content		
	lean	moist to medium	oily
Salmon			
Red King (Chinook)		x	
White King (Chinook)			x
Red (Sockeye)		x	
Pink		x	
Silver (Coho)		x	
Chum (Dog)		x	
Sea Bass	x		
Shark	x		
Sturgeon		x	
Swordfish	x		
Tuna			x
Trout			
Cutthroat		x	
Rainbow		x	
Dolly Varden		x	
Steelhead			x

Comments

Many consider this the finest eating salmon.

Mako is considered the best eating of the sharks, but all shark requires marinating. *Caution:* If a shark is hooked, it must be soaked on the boat in a special brine solution or the meat will spoil.

Many say this tastes like veal.

I prefer swordfish sashimied (raw), but if cooked, it must be marinated or basted with ample oil and then barely cooked.

I confess—this is my favorite!

This is sea-run trout and the best runs are in the winter; the meat and taste are similar to salmon.

Hawaiian Fish

Fish	Fat Content		
	lean	moist to medium	oily
Goatfish			
Kumu*		x	
Weke-ula		x	
Weke		x	
Mahimahi*		x	
Snappers			
Onaga* (Red Snapper)		x	
Opakapaka* (Pink Snapper)		x	
Uku (Gray Snapper)		x	

* These fish are considered the elite of the Hawaiian fish. There are many smaller Hawaiian fish which are very fine eating, but with an eye for simplicity, white meat, few bones, and practicality, I have not included them. In addition, I have omitted the aku and ahi (tuna) from the list, since I prefer tuna *only* sashimied. They are mentioned in the recipe for sashimi.

Comments

A beautiful red fish with firm white meat; ranges in size from ½ pound to 3½ pounds.

Another pretty red fish with some golden tints. While it is similar to kumu, it is not considered to be as delicate. I love it, and it is less expensive. Ranges from 1 to 4 pounds.

A small fish with soft white meat; it is more bony than the larger fish. Best steamed.

This is an excellent larger fish with delicate white meat and firm texture. Although this fish is a dolphin, it is not to be confused with our friend the porpoise. It is much, much smaller, has a different head, and reflects brilliant hues of rainbow colors when first caught.

A superb fish with firm white meat. It is prized for its sashimi quality and ranges in size from 1 to 20 pounds.

Excellent, delicate meat; very popular in the Islands, and its size is the same as onaga.

An underrated fish and usually a better buy. Firm white meat. Size is about the same as other snappers, but I've had good luck in finding larger ones which will serve 12.

Hawaiian Fish, continued

Fish	Fat Content		
	lean	moist to medium	oily
Rock Cod	x		
Muu (Porgy)		x	
Ono (Wahoo)*	x		
Papio*	x		x
Ulua			x
Shark	x		
Swordfish	x		
Sea Bass			

Comments

A firm white flesh prized for soups and steaming. I've also found it good fried.

A fine fish with white meat; prepare as though it were a snapper or goatfish.

The taste and texture falls between a swordfish and a mahimahi, although it is not quite as firm.

Dark, firm flesh similar to a mackerel; a baby Jack Crevally.

A full-size Jack Crevally; dark flesh.

Mako is considered the best eating, but all shark requires marinating. *Caution*: If a shark is hooked, it must be soaked on the boat in a special brine solution or the meat will spoil.

I prefer swordfish sashimied, but if cooked, it needs to be marinated or basted with ample oil and then barely cooked.

Steamed, Poached, and Baked

Oven-Steamed Kumu with Capers and Wine

First of all, don't let the length of this recipe throw you. This is really easy. Here are a few tips. Have the fishmonger clean, scale, and bone the fish by removing the backbone, yet leave the fish whole and intact, including the head. This is a neat trick, and if I attempted it, the poor fish would look like it had been on a dartboard. Some fishmongers may not know how to perform this artistic surgery or not be willing to perform it. If not, don't worry; just have him clean and scale the fish. It tastes divine either way. This entrée is particularly good for entertaining. I do all of the slicing and chopping in advance. I make the Butter-Wine Sauce before my guests arrive, prepare the fish, and preheat the oven. As my first guest arrives, I pop the fish into the oven and set the timer for half of the finished time.

Kumu   one 4- to 5-pound before dressing, or 3- to 4-pound dressed
Salt and white pepper   to taste
Butter-Wine Sauce (see Index)   ¾ cup
Medium onion   1, thinly sliced
Lemons   2, thinly sliced
Capers   2 tablespoons drained (reserve juice for sauce)
Parsley   garnish
Capers   garnish
Pimiento-stuffed green olive   garnish (optional)
Cucumber slices   garnish (optional)

Preheat oven to 300°. Quickly rinse fish in cold, running water and blot dry. Place fish on an ovenproof platter. Lightly salt and pepper the cavity. If the backbone has been removed, the fish will open easily to expose 2 halves. If the backbone has not been removed, make 3 diagonal slashes on top side of fish, about ½-inch deep, 2 inches apart. Pour half of sauce into cavity of fish and over top of fish. Using half of onion and lemon slices, arrange alternating rows inside cavity. Sprinkle capers over onions and lemons in cavity and pour remaining sauce over layers and again over top. Cover platter tightly with foil and place in oven. If cleaned fish is under 3 pounds, allow 15 minutes per pound; if over 3 pounds, allow 20 minutes per pound. A 3-pound cleaned kumu without backbone will take around 45 minutes. With backbone, add another 10 minutes. Halfway through time allowed, baste fish with juices. Do *not* turn fish. Re-cover fish and cook for remaining time. Test for doneness by inserting toothpick in thickest part of fish. Toothpick should meet minimum resistance, and meat should have lost translucence. When fish is done, remove foil, baste again with warm juices. With remaining onion and lemon slices, place 2 large onion slices and 3 lemon slices on top of fish, slightly overlapping edges, and arrange remaining slices around fish. Sprinkle lots of capers over fish. Add clumps of fresh green parsley either around fish or in one corner of platter. Cucumber slices also add a nice touch. If the eye of the fish offends you, place a small clump of parsley over it or cut 3 slices of a pimiento-stuffed green olive and arrange olive slices in triangular shape over the eye. Serves 6.

Fish Substitutions:
>   Pacific-Atlantic: salmon, red snapper, bluefish, pike
>   Hawaiian: opakapaka, weke-ula, uku, muu

Baked Fish with Spinach Stuffing

Fish   one 8- to 10-pound before dressing, or 6- to 7-pound dressed
Spinach Stuffing
Butter   3 tablespoons, melted
Dry white wine   3 tablespoons
Salt and pepper   to taste

Fill fish with stuffing and skewer closed. Place fish in large foil boat in large roasting pan and brush with melted butter and wine. Sprinkle with salt and pepper. Cover tightly and bake at 300° for 1 to 1½ hours, or until fish is done in thickest part. Serves 12.

Spinach Stuffing

Butter   4 tablespoons
Shallots   3 tablespoons finely chopped
Fresh spinach   1 bunch or ½ pound, cooked
Fresh bread crumbs   2½ cups
Heavy cream   3 tablespoons
Lemon juice   1 teaspoon
Salt   1½ teaspoons
Freshly ground pepper   to taste
Macadamia nuts   ½ cup chopped (optional)

In heavy skillet melt butter and cook shallots. Add spinach to evaporate most of moisture. Combine all ingredients in food processor and coarsely blend. Makes approximately 4⅔ cups.

Baked Fish with Shrimp–Bacon Stuffing

Fish one 3- to 4-pound before dressing, or 2-pound dressed
Shrimp–Bacon Stuffing
Bacon 1 or 2 slices, uncooked
Dry white wine (optional)
Green pepper rings garnish

Stuff the cavity of fish and lay 1 or 2 slices of uncooked bacon over the top. Place fish in a greased baking dish or on greased foil. Bake uncovered at 400° for about 15 to 20 minutes, basting occasionally with juices from pan or with white wine, or until fish is done in thickest portion. Garnish and serve immediately. Serves 4.

Shrimp–Bacon Stuffing

Shrimp ¼ cup shelled and deveined
Bacon 2 slices, fried crisp and broken into bits
Large mushroom 1, chopped
Parsley 1 tablespoon minced
Onion 1 teaspoon chopped
Green pepper 1 tablespoon chopped
Celery with leaves 1 tablespoon chopped
Salt ¼ teaspoon
White pepper ⅛ teaspoon
Thyme ⅛ teaspoon
Allspice ⅛ teaspoon
Nutmeg ⅛ teaspoon
Beau monde ¼ teaspoon
Bacon fat 1½ teaspoons
Butter 1½ teaspoons

Combine first 13 ingredients in food processor and coarsely blend. Heat bacon fat and butter together and sauté entire mixture over medium-low heat, stirring constantly. Taste for seasoning and correct if necessary. Makes approximately ¾ cup.

Baked Fish with Crab Stuffing

Fish   one 5- to 7-pound before dressing, or 4- to 5-pound dressed
Crab Stuffing
Salt and pepper   to taste
Sherry*   3 tablespoons
Lemon juice   1 tablespoon

Stuff fish and skewer closed. Place fish on ovenproof platter or in large foil boat in roasting pan. Salt and pepper and pour sherry and lemon juice over fish. Close foil tightly and bake at 300° for 1¼ hours, basting occasionally, or until fish is done in thickest part. Serves 8.
* You may substitute vermouth or white wine for the sherry.

Crab Stuffing

Crab   6-ounce can, drained and flaked
Parsley-Garlic Mix (see Index)   1 tablespoon
Bread crumbs   ½ cup
Salt and pepper   to taste
Thyme   ½ teaspoon
Sherry   enough to moisten

Combine all ingredients, adding just enough sherry to moisten stuffing. Makes approximately 1¼ cups.

Baked Fish with Pesto Stuffing

Fish   two 1½-pound each before dressing, or 1-pound each dressed
Salt and pepper   to taste
Pesto Stuffing
Dry white wine   ¼ cup

Place fish side by side in greased baking dish or foil, salt and pepper, and stuff. Skewer if necessary. Sprinkle white wine over fish, close foil tightly, and bake at 300° for 25 to 30 minutes, basting once. Serves 2.

Pesto Stuffing

Bacon croutons   ½ cup minced or
    Fine bread crumbs   ½ cup
Pesto Sauce (see Index)   4 tablespoons

Run croutons through food processor and toss with sauce. Makes ¾ to 1 cup.

Baked Opakapaka with Spinach Stuffing

Sheldon Zane is epicurean by nature and has the hefty size and good-natured smile that go with it. Each year he and his wife, Gwen, travel to France where Sheldon explores the wines and inns of a particular region. In fact, he developed many of the recipes in this book with a French surtitle. However, his repertoire is not limited to French cuisine, and he does equally well with the Hawaiian fish. Here is his recipe for a large opakapaka, but any fish normally served whole may be used.

Opakapaka   one 8- to 10-pound before dressing, or 6- to 7-pound dressed
Spinach Stuffing (see Index)   4⅔ cups
Butter   6 tablespoons, melted
Salt and pepper   to taste
Dry white wine   1 to 1¼ cups, depending upon size of fish
Butter   1 tablespoon, softened
Parsley   garnish
Pimiento-stuffed green olive   garnish
Lemon slices   garnish

Preheat oven to 400°. Quickly rinse fish and dry thoroughly. Fill fish with stuffing. Brush 2 tablespoons melted butter on bottom of ovenproof platter or foil boat, placing boat in roasting pan. Brush top of fish with remaining melted butter and salt and pepper it. Combine softened butter with wine and pour around fish. Bring fish to simmer on top of stove, then bake uncovered on middle shelf of oven, basting every 10 minutes with juices. Cook 1 to 1½ hours until fish is done in thickest part. Garnish with parsley clumps, sliced olive for the eye, and lemon slices. Serves 12.

The Mayonnaise Cure

Have you heard of the "mayonnaise cure"? Well, it does marvels for a baked fish, particularly if you're in a hurry. There are any number of interesting blends and combinations, but here are a few. Have some fun and devise your own.

Baked Fish with Shrimp–Curry Cure

Mayonnaise   4 tablespoons
Curry powder   2 teaspoons
Lemon juice   ½ teaspoon
Parsley   1 teaspoon minced
Jumbo shrimp   4, shelled and deveined
Fish   one 3- to 4-pound before dressing, or 2-pound dressed
Dry white wine   ½ cup (optional)

Mix all ingredients except shrimp and fish. Spread mixture thoroughly in cavity and on top of fish. (If there should be an insufficient amount to fully cover top, cover remaining area with oil.) Arrange shrimp inside cavity, allowing 1 to 2 shrimp per person. Bake uncovered in greased dish in 400° oven for 15 to 20 minutes, basting occasionally with juices or with wine, or place fish in foil. Pour wine over fish, cover tightly, and bake at 300°, basting once, for 30 minutes. Serves 4.

Baked Fish with Florentine Mask

Mayonnaise   5 tablespoons
Spinach   4 tablespoons blanched and minced
Onion   1 teaspoon diced
Bacon bits   2 teaspoons
Fish fillets or steaks   2 to 3 pounds
Bacon croutons   3 tablespoons crushed or
      Bread crumbs   3 tablespoons
Butter   1 tablespoon, melted

Combine mayonnaise, spinach, onion, and bacon bits in food processor or by hand. Mask fish with spinach mixture and sprinkle croutons mixed with butter over top. Bake in 350° oven for 20 to 30 minutes, until fish is tender. Finish browning under broiler if necessary. Serves 8.
Variation: To transform this from Florentine Mask to Watercress Cure, substitute minced watercress for spinach and 1 teaspoon lemon juice for the melted butter.

Baked Fish with Caper Cure

Fish one 3- to 4-pound before dressing, or 2-pound dressed
Mayonnaise 4 tablespoons
Capers 3 tablespoons chopped
Caper juice ½ teaspoon
Lemon juice ½ teaspoon
Parsley 1 teaspoon minced
Pimiento-stuffed green olives 3, chopped
Dry white wine ¼ cup

Make 2 diagonal slashes on top of fish, about ¼-inch deep. Combine all ingredients and mask entire fish with spread, including cavity and top side of fish. Sprinkle white wine over fish and bake in 400° oven for 15 to 20 minutes in greased pan or foil. Serves 4.

Baked Fish with Anchovy Cure

Mayonnaise 4 tablespoons
Anchovy paste 2 teaspoons
Parsley 1 teaspoon minced
Lemon juice ½ teaspoon
Anchovies 4, chopped
Fish one 3- to 4-pound before dressing, or 2-pound dressed
Dry white wine ¼ cup

Blend all ingredients except anchovies and fish. Mask fish with mixture, including cavity and top of fish. Sprinkle chopped anchovies inside cavity and pour white wine over fish. Bake uncovered in 400° oven in greased pan or foil for 15 to 20 minutes, or place fish on foil, cover tightly, and bake at 300°, basting once, for 30 minutes. Serves 4.

Poached Salmon with Hollandaise Sauce

Poaching is a delightful method for cooking fish because the low heat and self-basting action keep the fish delicate and moist. My husband's grandmother used to poach the tail of a salmon (the rear third of a salmon might be a better phrasing), saying that was the sweetest meat. Traditionally, she served it with a white sauce and it was always a special meal.

Court-Bouillon (see Index)   1 quart
Salmon   one 4-pound dressed, or 2⅔ pounds of steaks or fillets
Simple Hollandaise Sauce (see Index)   1½ cups

Prepare bouillon for fish. If using a whole salmon, gently wrap fish in clean cheesecloth or muslin (I bundle it like an old sheet, just tying all corners together), unless using a professional poacher; in that case, grease tray. For steaks or fillets, I recommend making individual poaching papers from parchment (just crimp the edges of the paper tightly and be sure your poaching "pillow" has room for air, as well as a cut center vent). If poaching steaks or a smaller slab, begin poaching when bouillon is at boiling point and immediately reduce heat to simmer and cover. Partially vent to allow some steam to escape. If poaching a whole fish or a large piece, permit bouillon to cool to room temperature before adding fish. Bring bouillon to boil, cover, and reduce heat to simmer. It is not necessary to vent a large slab or whole fish. Allow about 5 to 8 minutes per pound from the moment bouillon boils. Drain, gently remove cheesecloth or parchment pillow, and serve immediately with sauce. Serves 8.
Variation: Two delicious alternatives to Hollandaise are Mousseline Sauce and Beurre Blanc Sauce (see Index). Poached salmon is also excellent cold, particularly when it has been skinned and garnished. Serve with a cold sauce such as Chilled Cucumber Sauce or Green Mayonnaise (see Index).
Fish Substitutions:
    Pacific-Atlantic: pike, bass, snapper, sole, bluefish
    Hawaiian: kumu, onaga, opakapaka, bluerunner

Chilled Poached Whole Salmon

Jellied Consommé
Court-Bouillon (see Index)   to cover fish
Salmon*   one 8- to 10-pound before dressing, or 6- to 8-pound dressed
Pimiento-stuffed green olive   garnish
Parsley   garnish
Lemon slices   garnish
Cucumber slices   garnish
Deviled eggs   3 or 4, garnish (optional)
Green Mayonnaise (see Index)   2 cups

Prepare Jellied Consommé in advance. Then prepare bouillon to completely cover fish and cool. Wrap fish in cheesecloth if not using a poacher and rack. If using a rack, grease it. Bring bouillon to a boil and insert fish. Lower to simmer and cover. Poach about 7 to 8 minutes per pound. (For a 4- to 5-pound fish, allow 5 to 6 minutes per pound.) Drain, open cheesecloth, and slide fish onto serving platter. Leaving head and tail intact, skin and trim rest of fish, removing fins and gray, oily film until pink flesh shows. When fish has chilled, arrange consommé cutouts over body of fish. Cover eye of fish with stuffed olive and surround fish with parsley, lemon, and cucumber and several deviled eggs, if desired. Serve well chilled with Green Mayonnaise. Serves 12.
* If you lack the necessary equipment to poach an 8-pound fish, then poach two 5-pound fish.

Jellied Consommé*

Unflavored gelatin   1 envelope
Water   2 tablespoons
Beef consomme   1¼ cups undiluted, hot

Soften gelatin in water and dissolve in hot consommé. Pour into a large, shallow container and place in freezer for 40 minutes or in refrigerator for 4 hours. When jellied, cut into desired shapes with cookie cutters.
* Jellied Consommé will melt if placed on hot or warm food.

Classic Seafood Combo*

I've heard that Scandinavians are an efficient lot, and if my friend Kris Allison is any example, they are one of the most organized people in the world. She can wear a hard hat and direct the building of a home during the day and that evening serve a sumptuous dinner. Just plain disgusting, isn't it! Coming from Sweden, she has a natural affinity for seafood and is careful not to overwhelm it with stronger flavors. To serve this dish for company, have all ingredients measured and readily available. Serve with pilaf or wild rice and baked tomatoes provençale.

Mahimahi or swordfish   6 ounces, cubed
Shrimp   6 ounces, peeled, deveined, and halved lengthwise
Scallops   6 ounces, halved if large
Salt and white pepper   to taste
Garlic clove   1, squeezed
Butter   1 tablespoon
Olive oil   1 tablespoon
Parsley   ¼ teaspoon minced
Lemon peel spice   ¼ teaspoon
Dry white wine   ½ cup
Cream   ½ cup
Arrowroot   1 teaspoon
Dijon mustard   1 teaspoon
Dill weed   garnish
Cayenne   garnish
Lemon wedges   garnish

Season fish with salt and white pepper. Sauté garlic in butter and oil; add fish and sauté over low heat for 3 minutes. Add parsley, lemon peel spice, white wine, and cream. Mix arrowroot with mustard in a little bit of water—just enough to make a paste. Stir into fish mixture carefully. (Do not bring to a boil, because arrowroot will go thin again.) Pour mixture into preheated dish or serving tray and garnish with minced dill weed and a touch of cayenne. Serve with lemon wedges. Serves 4.
* As long as the meat is firm, any combination of fish and shellfish is workable.

Sole with Shrimp Sauce au Gratin

This is another of my Swedish friend's specialties. She prefers this for company since it is made ahead of time and refrigerated.

Court-Bouillon (see Index) 1¼ cups
Salt to taste
Sole fillets 8 small ones, about 2 pounds
White wine 2 tablespoons
Butter 3 tablespoons
Flour 2 tablespoons
Cooking liquid 1 cup, reserved and cooled
Whipping cream ⅓ cup
Tarragon ½ teaspoon
Salt and white pepper to taste
Tiny cooked shrimp 1 pound
Fine bread crumbs 1 cup, buttered

Prepare bouillon and strain. Salt fish and fold fillets in thirds. Place in single layer in 8-inch square baking dish. Sprinkle lightly again with salt and pour 1¼ cups of strained bouillon and wine over fish. Cover fish and bake for 20 minutes at 400°. Transfer fillets to individual dishes or shells and reserve 1 cup of hot cooking liquid. Allow it to cool. Melt butter in saucepan and add flour. Stir until tiny bubbles form, then add cooking liquid. Continue stirring until flour and butter are absorbed into liquid. Add cream and tarragon. Season with salt and white pepper. Remove from heat and add shrimp. Spoon sauce over fish in individual dishes or shells. Sprinkle bread crumbs over top, cover each dish, and refrigerate. When ready to serve, bake fish uncovered in preheated oven at 400° for 15 minutes or until bubbly and top is golden. Serves 8.
Fish Substitutions:
　　Pacific-Atlantic: salmon, snapper
　　Hawaiian: onaga, opakapaka, kumu

Enid's Eggs

Enid Wade is one of the finest gourmet cooks around, and many of us have been urging her to write her own cookbook. Her specialties are dishes which may be prepared in advance. In fact, this recipe demands that it must be made the night before, because it requires overnight refrigeration. Now that's my kind of dish!

Stale bread slices*   8
Butter   3 tablespoons
Sharp Cheddar cheese   2 cups grated
Eggs   3, beaten
Milk   2½ cups
Salt   1 teaspoon
Prepared mustard   ¼ teaspoon
Fresh crab   ¼ to ½ pound, cooked and flaked or
    Canned crab   6-ounce can, drained

The night before you plan to serve, gently butter both sides of bread slices. Place 4 slices of bread in 8-inch square buttered baking dish or pan. Beat eggs and add milk, salt, and mustard. Beat again until well mixed. Pour ½ mixture over the 4 slices of bread. Sprinkle ½ crab over eggs and top with ½ grated cheese. Place remaining 4 slices on top, and again add eggs topped with remaining crab and cheese. Cover and refrigerate. Bake uncovered at 325° for about 1 hour or a little longer, until eggs are nice and firm. Garnish with chopped parsley and paprika. Serves 6.
* Trim crusts from bread before it is stale, since it is more difficult to do once the bread is dry. Also, allow bread to get really hard and stale by cutting it one week in advance of serving it.
Variations: Some tasty alternatives to the crab filling are salmon, shrimp, ham, diced chilies, green pepper, or mushrooms.

Cantonese Steamed Mullet

Soy sauce 1¾ teaspoons
Spañada or sherry 1 teaspoon
Lemon peel ⅛ teaspoon grated
Garlic clove 1, pressed
Ground ginger ⅛ teaspoon
Chung choi* ½ ball, rinsed and chopped
Fresh coriander ½ teaspoon minced
Mullet one 1-pound dressed
Peanut oil 2 tablespoons
Fresh coriander or green onion garnish

Mix first 7 ingredients, stir thoroughly, and set aside. Place fish on platter in which it will be steamed and make 3 diagonal slashes on top side of fish. Spread mixture evenly over top of fish and in cavity. Pour water into large pot with rack, adding only enough water to boil without hitting rack. Place platter with fish on rack and bring water to a boil. Reduce heat to low, cover tightly, and steam for about 10 minutes, depending upon thickness of fish. (Allow 10 minutes for every inch of thickness.) When done, remove pot from heat and allow to stand covered for 5 minutes. Remove platter and set aside. In small pan, heat oil until it is smoking. Standing back, pour hot, sizzling oil over fish. Garnish with chopped coriander or sliced green onions. Serve immediately. Serves 4.
* Rinse chung choi to remove excess salt before chopping.
Fish Substitutions:
    Pacific-Atlantic: salmon, red snapper, rockfish
    Hawaiian: rock cod, kumu, weke, onaga

Steamed Mullet 4-Mile Style

When Sheldon Zane was growing up in Hilo on the Big Island, he recalls a place known as 4 Miles. There, tiny ponds were filled with lively mullet, and a restaurant specialized in catching and preparing your order. Talk about fresh fish! This is his memory of how it was prepared.

Mullet   4, approximately 1 pound each before dressing
Rock salt   to taste
Lemons   2, sliced
Green ti leaves   8 nice size, rinsed (more if small)
Water   ¾ cup
White wine   ¾ cup
Steamed white rice
Soy sauce

Rinse fish under cold water and pat dry. Score fish with sharp knife in Xs. Rub fish with rock salt and place each fish lengthwise in a ti leaf. Arrange lemon slices the length of fish on one side only. Wrap mullet with another large ti leaf (or more if necessary) and tie with string. Bring water mixed with white wine to a boil. Place wrapped mullet over, not in, the steaming water. Cover and steam for 15 minutes. Snip string and serve mullet hot in ti leaf with steamed white rice and soy sauce. Serves 4.
Note: If you lack a large enough poaching pan, you can place two racks in a broiler pan, bring the water to a boil, place wrapped fish on racks, and cover with foil. Bake at 400°.
Fish Substitutions:
    Pacific-Atlantic: small salmon, snapper
    Hawaiian: weke, kumu, onaga

Poached Sole with Bercy Sauce

Sole fillets   ¾ pound
Anchovy paste   to cover
Butter   1 tablespoon
Shallots   1 teaspoon minced
Dry white wine   ½ cup
Parsley   1 teaspoon minced
Salt   ¼ teaspoon
Cayenne   ⅛ teaspoon
Velouté Sauce (see Index)   ½ cup
Parsley   garnish
Lemon slices   garnish

Spread thin layer of anchovy paste over fillets. In Dutch oven or frying pan, melt butter and add shallots. Sauté over medium heat. Add wine, parsley, salt, and cayenne. Stir until salt dissolves and lower heat to simmer. Lay fillets in poaching liquid, cover, and simmer for 2 minutes. Using a spatula, carefully turn fillets, replace lid, and simmer another 2 or 3 minutes. (Fish other than sole will need to cook for 5 minutes.) Place fillets on warmed platter. Add sauce to poaching liquid, stir until warmed, then pour over fish. Garnish with more parsley and lemon slices. Serves 2.

Variation: If you do not have Velouté Sauce on hand, either fresh or frozen, you may use Beurre Manié (see Index).

Fish Substitutions:
    Pacific-Atlantic: salmon, snapper, bluefish
    Hawaiian: kumu, weke, weke-ula, opakapaka

Escalloped Oyster Casserole

Connie Hereford's family has had this recipe for at least four generations. It originated in Nonquitt, Massachusetts, on the Cape. She serves it as a side dish with roast turkey on holidays.

Saltine cracker crumbs 2 cups
Salt ½ teaspoon
Pepper dash
Butter ½ cup, melted
Oysters* 1 pint, drained, liquor reserved
Oyster liquor plus heavy cream 1 cup
Heavy cream 1 cup
Worcestershire sauce ¼ teaspoon

Combine crackers, salt, pepper, and melted butter in bowl. Layer ⅓ of cracker mix in a buttered 8 by 4½-inch baking dish. Chop oysters into large pieces and layer ½ of them. Next, add another ⅓ of cracker mix, followed by remaining oysters. Reserve remaining cracker mix. (You may refrigerate at this point if making in advance.) Pour in 1 cup oyster liquor plus heavy cream, then 1 cup heavy cream combined with Worcestershire sauce. Top with remaining cracker crumbs and bake at 350° for 30 minutes. Serves 4 as main dish or 6 as side dish.

* You may substitute freshly shucked oysters if desired.

Note: If you double the recipe, reduce the amount of cracker crumbs.

Snapper in Mustard and Wine

This dish works equally well with fillets of sole. My husband, who prefers hot dishes, adds more tabasco.

Dry white wine   ½ cup
Butter   2 tablespoons
Lemon juice   1 tablespoon
Dijon mustard   2 tablespoons
Sugar   ⅛ teaspoon
Garlic clove   1, pressed
Tabasco   2 drops
Rock salt and white pepper   to taste
Snapper fillets   ¾ pound
Beurre Manié (see Index)   1½ teaspoons or
   Cornstarch   1½ teaspoons
Parsley   garnish
Lemon wedges   garnish

Mix first 7 ingredients. Microwave at 70% for 1 minute; stir and microwave again at 70% for another minute. (Or heat over stove until butter melts and ingredients are blended.) Rub rock salt into fillets and pepper lightly. Place fillets in 8-inch square glass baking dish and pour sauce over fish. Cover with waxed paper and microwave for 3 minutes at 70%. With spatula, rotate fish and microwave for 4 more minutes. (Or poach in covered pan on stove for 10 minutes.) Thicken stock with Beurre Manié and pour over fish on warmed platter. Sprinkle with minced parsley and serve immediately with lemon wedges. Serves 2 to 3.
Fish Substitutions:
   Pacific-Atlantic: sole, salmon, rockfish
   Hawaiian: ono, weke, rock cod

Cajun Fish Rolls

My family likes this dinner, and I like it because it is easy, quick, and looks and tastes good. I usually make a southern night of it by serving canned turnip greens (or mustard greens or spinach), cooked with bacon and flavored with vinegar. Add baked potatoes with sour cream and chives and you have an attractive, simple meal.

Sole fillets   1 pound
Cajun Sauce (see Index)*   ½ cup
Boiled ham   4-ounce package, sliced
Swiss cheese   4-ounce package, sliced or grated

Place fillets in 8-inch square glass baking dish. Cut any particularly ....₀ fillets in half. Drizzle ¾ teaspoon of sauce over each fillet. Trim a piece of ham and a piece of cheese to fit center section of each fillet. Fold over the two ends and secure with toothpick. Pour remaining sauce over fish. Cover dish with waxed paper and microwave for 5 minutes at 70%. Gently turn rolls so that inside rolls are now on outside edge of dish. Microwave for another 5 minutes at 70%. (Or cover with foil and bake in preheated conventional oven at 325° for 20 minutes.) To serve, spoon sauce over each roll and pour remaining sauce into small serving bowl. Serves 4.

* You may make the sauce early and set aside at room temperature.

Fish Substitutions:
   Pacific-Atlantic: snapper, haddock, sea bass, lingcod, rockfish
   Hawaiian: shark, ono, sea bass, rock cod

Baked Turbot with Wheat Germ

This dish particularly drew the applause of my children. It is indeed refreshing to serve them something which they enjoy that is thoroughly nourishing!

Turbot fillets   1 pound
Vegetable oil   ½ cup
Garlic clove   1, pressed
Paprika   ½ teaspoon
Salt   ¼ teaspoon
Untoasted wheat germ*   ½ cup

Grease a shallow 8-inch square baking pan. Combine oil and seasonings in bowl and beat vigorously with fork or whisk. Using a pastry brush, brush both sides of fillets with oil mixture. Roll fillets on both sides in wheat germ and place in baking pan. Dab each fillet again with remaining sauce. Bake in preheated 400° oven for 20 to 25 minutes, or until wheat germ has browned. Serve with your favorite sauce. Serves 4.

* If toasted wheat germ is used, reduce cooking time to 10 minutes.

Fish Substitutions:
   Pacific-Atlantic: snapper, sole, rockfish, bluefish
   Hawaiian: rock cod, uku, taape

Sole with Asparagus and Onion Rings

This is one of my favorites. It's so easy to make and deliciously elegant for entertaining. When I make it for our family, I use only a pound of sole, yet make all the sauce, and serve it with lemon wedges, sliced tomatoes, and pilaf.

Sole fillets*   2 pounds
Salt and white pepper   ½ teaspoon
Frozen asparagus spears   10-ounce package or
    Canned asparagus spears   10-ounce can
Condensed cream of celery soup   10¾-ounce can
Lemon juice   1 tablespoon
Worcestershire sauce   1 teaspoon
French-fried onion rings   3-ounce can
Parmesan cheese   2 tablespoons grated
Parsley   garnish

Sprinkle fillets with salt and pepper. Cook asparagus until barely tender (omit cooking for canned asparagus). Arrange 3 to 4 asparagus spears on each fillet, roll fish around them, and secure with toothpick if necessary. Place fillets in 8-inch square baking dish (greased if baking in conventional oven). Combine soup, lemon juice, Worcestershire sauce, and ½ onion rings and spoon over fish rolls. Sprinkle with cheese. (If preparing ahead, this may now be covered and refrigerated.) Microwave at 70% for 10 minutes. Gently turn rolls so that inner sides face outward, sprinkle remaining onion rings over top, and microwave at 70% additional 8 minutes. (For conventional oven, bake uncovered at 350° for 20 to 25 minutes, adding remaining onion rings during last 5 minutes.) Garnish with finely chopped parsley. Serves 8.
* The longer, larger fish fillets need to be cut in half.
Fish Substitutions:
    Pacific-Atlantic: salmon, snapper
    Hawaiian: opakapaka, weke-ula, uku

Bass Baked in Greek Bouillabaisse Sauce

The traditional bouillabaisse is a time-consuming dish to prepare and a very expensive one. This hybrid version of bouillabaisse sauce with sea bass steaks comes from an idea of Donna Hicks, my dental hygienist. I suppose picking one's teeth usually conjures images of eating, so while she cleans my molars we talk about food.

Sea bass steaks six ½-pound each
Fresh lemon juice ¼ cup
Salt 1 teaspoon
Coarsely ground black pepper ¼ teaspoon
Leek 1, white portion only, rinsed, cut in 1-inch sections and julienned
Celery 1 stalk, minced
Medium tomatoes 2, peeled and chopped
Parsley-Garlic Mix (see Index) 2 tablespoons or
    Parsley 2 tablespoons chopped and
    Garlic cloves 2, pressed
Olive oil 3 tablespoons
Ground savory ¼ teaspoon
Thyme ¼ teaspoon
Salt ¼ teaspoon
Pickapeppa Sauce 1 teaspoon
Dry white wine ¾ cup
Fresh mint leaves 5, minced
Orange rind ¼ teaspoon grated or minced
Thick tomato slices 6
Parsley 1 tablespoon finely chopped
Fine bread crumbs ¼ cup
Butter 3 tablespoons, melted

Marinate steaks in lemon juice, 1 teaspoon salt, and pepper in a covered 8-inch square glass baking dish for 1 hour. In large skillet, sauté leek, celery, tomatoes, and Parsley-Garlic Mix in olive oil over medium heat for about 3 minutes. Stir in savory, thyme, ¼ teaspoon salt, and Pickapeppa Sauce. Pour in wine and add mint leaves and orange rind. Simmer uncovered over medium heat, stirring frequently, until sauce thickens, about 20 to 30 minutes. Allow sauce to cool. Pour sauce directly over fish steaks. Arrange a tomato slice on each steak and sprinkle slices with parsley. Mix bread crumbs with melted butter and evenly divide crumbs to cover lightly each tomato slice. Bake uncovered for 20 minutes in preheated 350° oven. If necessary, brown bread crumbs quickly under broiler before serving. Serves 6.

Fish Substitutions:
    Pacific-Atlantic: halibut, pike, cod, scrod
    Hawaiian: mahimahi, opakapaka, ono, uku

Mahimahi–Halibut Supreme

This is an excellent dish for those nights when you know he (or she) is tired or down, when you want to serve something special, something attractive, something that says yes, you care, and that allows quick preparation. In fact, this recipe is so special that it's worth investing in the best ripe tomatoes you can find, perhaps the hothouse variety. My favorite companions to this entrée are sautéed Quartered Mushrooms, Potatoes Anna, and a green salad.

Parsley-Garlic Mix (see Index)   2 teaspoons
Fine bread crumbs   ½ teaspoon
Mayonnaise   2 tablespoons
Curry powder   ½ teaspoon
Mahimahi or halibut steaks   2
Fresh dill   ½ teaspoon minced (optional)
Swiss cheese   2 teaspoons grated
Tomato slices   two, ½-inch thick
Salt   to taste

Prepare Parsley-Garlic Mix, blend with bread crumbs, and set aside. Mix mayonnaise and curry powder and spread approximately 1 tablespoon of mixture on each steak. Sprinkle dill over steaks. Then sprinkle grated cheese over each steak and top with tomato slices. Lightly salt tomato slices and spread 1 teaspoon Parsley-Garlic Mix over each slice. Cover and microwave on high for 4 minutes. Turn fish and microwave additional 2 minutes if needed. (For conventional oven, bake uncovered at 350° for 20 minutes.) Serves 2.
Note: If you are microwaving more than 2 steaks, rotate steaks after 3 minutes and microwave another 3 minutes. If you should use swordfish, be certain to microwave no longer than 4 minutes total, and in a conventional oven bake covered.
Variations: You may substitute a seasoning of your choice for the curry powder. Some possibilities are mashed anchovies or anchovy paste, mashed capers, horseradish, or Pickapeppa Sauce. Or simply substitute tartar sauce for the seasoned mayonnaise.
Fish Substitutions:
   Pacific-Atlantic: salmon, black cod, swordfish, bluefish
   Hawaiian: kumu, swordfish, sea bass, ono

Bluefish–Watercress Soufflé

When I serve this to my family, I get lazy and use a packaged white sauce, adding an extra tablespoon of chopped watercress to the white sauce just before serving.

For company, I make the velouté and add Carottes Vichy and Potatoes Anna or kasha to round out a colorful meal.

Bluefish fillets 1 pound boned and skinned
Onion ¼ cup finely chopped
Fresh mushrooms ½ cup finely chopped
Watercress 1 cup finely chopped
Fresh red chili pepper ¾ teaspoon seeded and minced
Large egg 1
Fine bread crumbs 1 cup
Lemon juice 2 tablespoons
Beau monde 1 teaspoon
Parmesan cheese ½ cup grated
Salt ¾ teaspoon
White pepper ½ teaspoon
Heavy cream 1 cup
Boiling water 2 cups
Velouté Sauce (see Index) 2 cups
Watercress garnish
Radishes garnish

Blend first 13 ingredients in a food processor. Pour mixture into greased 1-quart soufflé dish, cover, and refrigerate at this point if making ahead. Otherwise, cover with waxed paper and set a heavy ovenproof plate over top. Preheat oven to 375°. Set dish inside a Dutch oven and pour boiling water around it. Bake 45 minutes to 1 hour, or until center is set. Test for doneness by inserting toothpick in middle; when soufflé is done, toothpick will appear almost clean. To serve, place serving tray over top of soufflé dish and, holding firmly, invert to unmold. Gently tap bottom of dish if necessary. Sprinkle warmed sauce with minced watercress and pour ½ sauce over soufflé. Serve remaining sauce on the side. Surround soufflé with rose-cut radishes. Serves 6.
Variation: Other possible garnishes are a large, thin orange slice sprinkled with minced lemon peel; a large, thin lemon slice sprinkled with paprika (or 3 smaller ones); or rose-cut radishes arranged on watercress leaves.
Note: If preparing this without a food processor, cut fish in small pieces and mix and mash ingredients by hand, as you would a meat loaf. Also, be sure to handle hot chili peppers with care. If you do not wear rubber gloves, avoid contact with eyes. Wash hands with soapy water as soon as finished with pepper.
Fish Substitutions:
Pacific-Atlantic: sole, sea bass, lingcod, rockfish, haddock, salmon
Hawaiian: sea bass, muu, ono, uku, weke-ula

Seafood Lasagna

For our last Christmas party, we asked Ed Greene, owner of Jameson's Merchant Square Oyster Bar, to cater the event. He and Warren Howard, the chef, did a splendid job. Warren also makes a delectable lasagna, and the whopping portion served in the downtown restaurant is fit for Paul Bunyan. When I serve this, I prepare the sauce (and yes, it does take ten garlic cloves) and mix and grate the cheeses the day before. Then the day I plan to serve it, I assemble and refrigerate it.

Italian Diablo Sauce   3 cups
Spinach-Mushroom Mix
Seafood Mix (see page 50)
Lasagna noodles*   8 ounces, cooked and drained
Swiss cheese   1¼ cups grated
Cheddar cheese   1¼ cups grated

Make Italian Diablo Sauce, Spinach-Mushroom Mix, and Seafood Mix 1 day in advance. Cook noodles, drain, and lay out ½, overlapping slightly, in an oiled 9 by 13-inch pan. (Be sure to use the best, unbroken noodles on the top.) With large, flat spoon, spread Seafood Mix, then 2 cups sauce, evenly over noodles. Next, sprinkle with 1 cup each of both cheeses. Then, distribute Spinach-Mushroom Mix in small spoonfuls and spread evenly. When smooth, top with remaining ½ noodles, overlapping slightly. Spread remaining 1 cup sauce over top and sprinkle with ¼ cup each of cheeses. Cover with foil and bake at 350° for 30 to 40 minutes (if refrigerated, bake 45 minutes). To serve, allow pan to sit for 10 to 15 minutes, then cut lasagna into serving portions. Serves 12.
* Choose only the best, unbroken noodles; discard rest.

Italian Diablo Sauce*

Garlic cloves 10
Parsley 1 tablespoon minced
Anchovies 1 ounce, drained
Small onion 1, chopped
Capers 1 tablespoon
Olive oil 2 tablespoons
White wine ¼ cup
Bay leaf 1
Oregano ¼ teaspoon
Crushed red pepper ¼ teaspoon
Tomato sauce 6 cups
Tomato paste one 6-ounce can
Parmesan cheese ½ cup grated

Blend first 7 ingredients in food processor. Sauté mixture lightly, add spices, and simmer for 5 minutes. Add tomato sauce and paste. Simmer uncovered, stirring occasionally, approximately 1½ hours and add cheese. Remove bay leaf and stir well. Makes 5 cups.
* The Italian Diablo Sauce recipe makes a sizable amount. Freeze unused portions or use with spaghetti or crepes.

Spinach-Mushroom Mix

Medium onion 1, diced
Mushrooms ¼ pound, sliced
Olive oil 1 tablespoon
Fresh spinach 1 pound, chopped, blanched, and squeezed or
    Frozen chopped spinach 10-ounce package, thawed and squeezed
Egg 1, slightly beaten
Dijon mustard 1 teaspoon
Parmesan cheese ¼ cup grated
Ricotta cheese 1 cup

Sauté onion and mushrooms in oil. Transfer to mixing bowl and add remaining ingredients. Mix well and set aside. Makes 3 cups.
Variation: Warren uses this mix to make a rich, special crepe. Fill crepe with mix and pour Mornay Sauce over; then top with a little Hollandaise Sauce (see Index).

Seafood Mix

Shrimp   ½ pound, peeled and deveined
Medium scallops   ½ pound, sliced
White fish fillets   ½ pound
Poaching liquid*   1¼ cups reserved and strained
Sherry   1 tablespoon
Parmesan cheese   ¼ cup grated
Roux (see Index)   1½ tablespoons flour mixed with 1½ tablespoons
    butter

Lightly poach shrimp, scallops, and fish, reserving poaching liquid. Cut fish into bite-sized chunks. In saucepan, combine strained poaching liquid, sherry, and cheese. Bring to boil and thicken with roux. Add cooked seafood to sauce and gently blend. Makes 3 cups.
* Add clam juice, water, or white wine, if necessary, to make 1¼ cups poaching liquid.
Variation: This superb seafood blend doubles as the filling used in Warren's cannelloni. Fill cannelloni (or crepe) with mix, pour Mornay Sauce over (see Index), and then pour a little of the Italian Diablo Sauce over that.
Note: If preparing Seafood Mix a day early, make sauce, but refrigerate seafood separately since seafood will leak water and weaken sauce.

Green Chili–King Salmon Bake

This dish serves nicely when you're asked to bring a casserole to a large potluck party; it's even nicer if you've caught the salmon yourself. Ahh, the stuff of which dreams are made.

Butter   3 tablespoons
Large green pepper   1, chopped
Large onion   1, chopped
Flour   3 tablespoons
Court-Bouillon (see Index)   1¼ cups strained and cooled
Green chilies   7-ounce can, drained, seeded, and diced
Garlic cloves   2, pressed or minced
Salmon   4 cups boned and skinned, sliced in 3 by 1-inch strips
Jack cheese   1 pound, shredded
Sour cream   1½ cups
Chilled Asparagus Topping
Hard-cooked egg yolks   garnish

Melt butter in frying pan and sauté green pepper and onion until onion is translucent. Sprinkle flour over vegetables, stir well, and cook until flour begins to bubble. Gradually add bouillon, stirring constantly until sauce thickens. Add green chilies and garlic to sauce and set aside. Lay ½ fish strips in 9 by 13-inch greased baking dish and salt to taste. Next sprinkle with ⅓ cheese and ½ sauce. Layer remaining fish, sprinkle with ⅓ cheese, and add remaining sauce. Cover top of casserole with sour cream and sprinkle with remaining cheese. (If making ahead, cover and refrigerate.) Preheat oven to 325° and bake uncovered for 1 hour (add additional 15 minutes to baking time if previously refrigerated). Allow casserole to sit 10 minutes before spooning over topping and garnishing with egg yolks. Serves 12.

Chilled Asparagus Topping

Asparagus tips   10-ounce can, drained
Pimientos   2, diced
Italian salad dressing   3 tablespoons, oil and vinegar variety

Gently toss asparagus tips and diced pimiento with dressing. (This can be made ahead and chilled.) Makes 1¼ cups.

Baked Squid with Pesto Stuffing

This is an easy family dinner and excellent for the tight budget at the end of the month. The hardest part is cleaning the squid early in the day (or the night before). Allow 3 squid per person, unless using jumbo squid, since the squid shrink in cooking. Actually, the shrinking exposes the stuffing, and it appears as though you had planned the whole appearance. The stuffed squid is delicious served with hot buttered noodles sprinkled with a bit of poppy seed and broccoli, cooked, then quickly sautéed in butter and sprinkled with Parmesan.

Cleaning the Squid

Cleaning the squid or cuttlefish, of course, might be unsettling for the novice. However, this is no time to be squeamish—just think of the price per pound, the minimal waste, the nutritional value, and you will do fine. When cleaning my first two, I turned my head to one side, squinted, and peeked with one eye. Now it's old hat, and it will be for you, too. I invariably clean the squid early in the day, then cover and refrigerate it until I'm ready to cook.

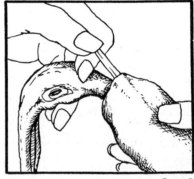

Step 1   Step 2

1. Under the cold-water tap, rub and pull off the speckled, purplish membrane. You will know when it is off because the white meat will be exposed.

2. Feel for and pull out the long, transparent sword from the hood. Discard it.

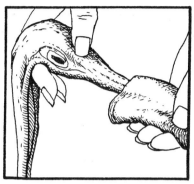
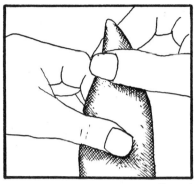

Step 3   Step 4

3. Gently pull the body from the hood, stripping off and discarding the viscera that easily separate from the body. This is easier than it sounds; sometimes the viscera come out with the sword.

4. Clean out the inside of the hood. Starting from the smaller end and moving your fingers toward the larger end, squeeze out the inner contents. Clean and rinse out. Often, I use a chopstick to scrape the lining. (When I cut rings, I check the inner portion again.) Set the cleaned hood on a plate.

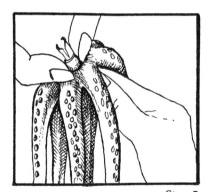

Step 5

5. Holding the body, pop out the beak from between the legs. Turn the body upside down, and with a squeezing and backward motion, pop the beak out with your fingers and discard it. Rinse the body and cut the tentacles if you plan to cook them. My husband likes the tentacles, but I still prefer the hood.

Squid (or cuttlefish)   12 cleaned, about 1.8 to 2 pounds
Pesto Stuffing (see Index) *   ¾ cup
Ragu Sauce   ¾ cup commercially bottled variety
White wine   ½ cup

Take white mantle and cut lengthwise through one side. Open and clean underlining; pat dry. Place 1 tablespoon of stuffing on each mantle. Close, barely overlapping edges. If jumbo species, just stuff without cutting. Place cut side up in 8-inch square baking dish. Mix sauce (preferably variety with mushrooms) with wine and spoon over stuffed squid. Cover and refrigerate if making ahead. Microwave on high for 10 minutes, if refrigerated, turning dish a quarter turn after 5 minutes. If not refrigerated, microwave on high for 8 minutes, turning dish after 4 minutes. (If not microwaving, simmer on stove or bake in 350° oven, covered, for about 20 minutes.) Serves 4.

* When making the stuffing, use the fine bread crumbs, because squid doesn't release the juices that a baked fish does, so the fine bread crumbs give a softer texture. You may make the Pesto Sauce called for in the stuffing several days in advance if you wish and, after the stuffing is made, use any leftover sauce in the Snapper with Pesto Sauce (see Index); just thin it with white wine. You may chop the tentacles and add those to the stuffing, but frankly, I don't. Sometimes I fry the tentacles the next day calamari-style for my husband.

Curried Haddock Casserole

Salt   1½ teaspoons
White pepper   ¾ teaspoon
Curry powder   1 tablespoon
Potatoes   1 pound, peeled and sliced
Carrots   1 cup peeled and thinly sliced
Onion   ½ cup diced
Celery   ½ cup diced
Haddock fillets   1 pound boned
Butter   3 tablespoons

Grease a deep baking dish and preheat oven to 425°. Mix salt, pepper, and curry powder. Layer ⅓ vegetables and sprinkle with portion of seasonings and parsley. Next, layer ⅓ fillets and dot with ½ tablespoon butter and sprinkle with seasonings. Continue forming layers, sprinkling with seasonings, parsley, and butter. Dot top with remaining butter, cover, and bake for 1 hour. (If casserole has been refrigerated after layering, add 15 minutes to baking time.) Garnish with remaining parsley. Serves 4 to 6.

Fish Substitutions:
   Pacific-Atlantic: sole, turbot, bluefish
   Hawaiian: fillets of butterfish, taape, weke, akule

Steamed Mussels

Mussels* 24
White wine 1½ cups
Water ½ cup
Parsley 2 tablespoons minced
Chervil 1 tablespoon
Shallots 2 tablespoons minced
Butter 3 tablespoons
Cayenne ⅛ to ¼ teaspoon, depending upon taste
Hot Garlic Butter (see Index) ½ cup

Mix everything but mussels in large Dutch oven. Place mussels on cake rack placed in Dutch oven. Bring mixture to a boil and cover to steam mussels until they open. Allow 15 minutes. Strain broth and pour over mussels placed in individual serving bowls. Serve with a small bowl of Hot Garlic Butter on the side. Serves 2.
* Mussels are steamed like clams, although they take less time. However, they have "beards" which must be scrubbed before steaming.

Oven-Steamed Oysters

My husband and I spent a memorable afternoon with friends in Dungeness. Roy had a special method for steaming oysters; they were plump, tender, and nobody had to shuck! He had five dozen fresh oysters, and three of us finished them off. Normally a chef allows a dozen if the oysters are the entrée and a half dozen if the oysters are an appetizer; but if you are serving true oyster lovers, allow more per person.

Oysters 48 in the shell
Hot Garlic Butter (see Index) 1 cup

Cover 2 oven racks with heavy-duty foil and heat oven to 500°. Place oysters on oven racks and close oven for 20 minutes. Open and remove those oysters whose shells have opened. For unopened oysters, close oven for another 10 to 15 minutes. Serve on large platter with garlic butter for dipping. Serves 4.
Note: I prefer either individual bowls for dipping or a bowl to be shared by 2 people, no more. A well-chilled white wine is definitely in order, such as a chablis, a grey riesling, or a dry semillon.

Konishi Kona Crab

Larry Konishi of Tamashiro Market told me he used to steam his crab until a Japanese chef prepared a boiled one for him. Now he does likewise. The boiling water apparently cleanses the crab of any grit and sand.

Large Kona crab*   1
Boiling water   large potful
Hot Garlic Butter (see Index)   ¼ cup

Place crab in large pot of boiling water. Be certain that its back is totally covered with water. Cook at full boil for 20 to 25 minutes, depending on size of crab. Drain. Break open back and remove food from its 3 partitions. Serve immediately or chilled with garlic butter. Serves 2.
* Kona crab is similar to Dungeness, but Kona crab flesh is firmer and sweeter and its legs not large enough for eating (but they are good for sucking). Kona crab is available in Hawaii only in the summer months.

East Coast Steamed Hard-Shell Crabs

Scallions and chili pepper add zest to the crabs in this recipe. Be sure to gauge your use of the chili pepper according to its strength and size.

Water   2-inch depth to cover bottom of pot
Salt   to taste
Scallions   3
Fresh small red chili pepper   1, sliced or
** Dried red chili pepper   1 tablespoon crushed**
Live hard-shell crabs   6 to 12
Hot Garlic Butter (see Index)   2 cups

Put 2 inches of water in a large, deep pot. Add salt, scallions, and chili pepper. Bring mixture to boil. Throw in live crabs, enough to cover bottom of pot. Cover and keep on low boil for 45 minutes. Serve with garlic butter or chill for later use. Serves 12.
Variations: Serve cold with a chilled sauce, such as Blender Aioli, Curry Mayonnaise, Chilled Cucumber, or Chilled Watercress Sauce (see Index).

Sautéed and Fried

Fried Trout with Bacon

Whenever my husband returns from a trip to Alaska, we have a large fish fry for the neighborhood. The favorite among guests is his Fried Trout with Bacon. This is how he does it. First he has a martini and a few laughs. Then he dons a large apron and brandishes a long-handled spatula. Next, he disappears into the kitchen, not to be seen or heard from again until he carries his delectable trout to the waiting table. Below is the recipe reduced to serve two people, but it is simple to multiply for a happy crowd.

Medium rainbow trout or small Dolly Varden trout or
    cutthroat trout*   2
Lemon juice   from 1 lemon
Salt and white pepper   to taste
Bacon   4 slices
Large garlic clove   1, minced
Scallions   2, chopped
Flour   ¼ cup
Parsley   garnish
Lemon wedges   garnish

Squeeze lemon juice inside and over trout and salt and pepper cavities. In large skillet, preferably cast-iron, cook bacon slices until crisp. Remove slices, drain, and set aside. Add garlic and scallions to skillet and cook until golden. Quickly roll trout in flour and shake off excess. Fry trout until both sides are golden over medium to medium-high heat. Turn trout only once, allowing about 5 minutes per side. To serve, remove trout to preheated platter. Crumble bacon slices over trout, along with garlic and scallions. Garnish with parsley and serve with lemon wedges Serves 2.
* There really is no fish which is a suitable substitute for trout, in my opinion. Islanders might try a small kumu, onaga, or weke, but these do not taste the same as fresh trout.

Trout with Almond Paste

This is truly a sublime dish. I use a small Japanese rice paddle (also known as "Mom's Fanny Paddle", in our house) for stuffing the fish, and even for turning the trout when sautéing. Just insert the paddle into the cavity and flip the trout over. And to round out the sublime, add sautéed mushrooms, tomatoes provençale, and potatoes au gratin to your feast of trout!

Rainbow trout or small cutthroat trout or small Dolly Varden trout*   4
Butter   3 tablespoons
Vegetable oil   1 tablespoon
Almond Paste

Preheat oven to 400° and pat trout dry. Heat large frying pan, preferably cast-iron. Add butter and oil and when butter starts to sizzle, sauté trout for 2 to 3 minutes over high heat, turning only once. Remove trout to ovenproof platter. Make Almond Paste and stuff each fish with it. Divide remaining paste over the body of each fish, beginning in gill area and arranging the paste toward tail. Place platter in oven and cook for 10 minutes. Serves 4.

* Again, there is no substitute for trout. However, this recipe would go well with a slightly larger fish, too, such as onaga or opakapaka in Hawaii, or even a smaller sockeye or silver salmon. If using a larger fish, allow 10 minutes for every inch of thickness.

Almond Paste

Unsalted butter*   ½ pound
Salt   1 teaspoon
Almonds   1 cup ground

Melt butter over medium to medium-high heat. Add salt and stir until salt dissolves. Next, add ground almonds, ¼ cup at a time, stirring into a thick paste. Do not let butter burn (the almonds do not need to cook). Once it is mixed, it is finished.

* If you use regular butter, decrease salt in recipe.

Trout Grenobloise

Whenever a friend wants to treat me for some special occasion, such as a birthday I'm no longer counting, I automatically think of Chez Michel French Restaurant in Honolulu. Chez Michel's is a very special place—bright flowers, ceramic tile, wicker furniture, and fine art all blend to form a sophisticated, yet relaxing atmosphere. And the food—the food is divine! Even though I always enter truly believing I will select a different entrée, I always order the same lunch. "Perhaps the tournedos today," I think, "or the ribs, or definitely the cannelloni." But when I review the menu, I invariably hear myself saying, "I'll have the Trout Grenobloise. . . ."

Trout   4
Salt and white pepper   to taste
Flour   ½ cup
Butter   2 tablespoons
Oil   1 tablespoon
Butter   2 tablespoons
Capers   ¼ cup
Parsley   ¼ cup chopped
Lemon slices   garnish
Paprika   dash
Parsley   garnish

Pat trout dry and lightly salt and pepper. Dust fish in flour and shake off excess. Heat large frying pan and add 2 tablespoons butter and oil. Sauté trout over medium-high heat, turning once, allowing about 5 minutes per side. Remove trout to preheated serving platter or plates. Drain remaining oil from frying pan. Melt 2 tablespoons butter, then add capers and ¼ cup parsley. Sauté and pour over trout. (Do not add any garlic or wine.) With sharp knife, peel lemon, leaving pulp intact. Then slice lemon in ⅛-inch to ¼-inch slices. Decorate half of each slice with paprika and the other half with minced parsley, placing the decorated lemon slices on top of trout. Serves 4.
Note: This goes very well with sautéed long beans and country-fried potatoes.

Michel's Frog Legs

Michel says to be certain to have only baby frog legs since the larger frog legs should be fried. This is my husband's favorite dish at Michel's, which, like my Trout Grenobloise, he usually orders.

Baby frog legs 12
Salt and pepper to taste
Flour ¼ cup
Butter 5 tablespoons
Garlic 2 teaspoons minced
Parsley 1 tablespoon chopped
White wine ¼ cup

Pat legs dry, salt and pepper, and roll in flour. Heat large frying pan, preferably cast-iron, over medium to medium-high heat. Add 2 tablespoons butter and when melted, sauté frog legs slowly, turning when light golden (about 5 to 7 minutes). When finished, remove legs to preheated platter or plates. Pour off browned butter and add remaining 3 tablespoons butter. Sauté garlic and parsley for a moment and add wine, stirring vigorously until sauce is well blended (about 1 minute). Pour sauce over frog legs and serve at once. Serves 2.

Fillets of Sole Meunière

This is a delightful dish for company—easy, quick, and elegant when served on a nice tray surrounded by small clumps of fresh parsley and lemon slices.

Fine bread crumbs 6 tablespoons
Flour 2 tablespoons
Salt and white pepper to taste
Sole fillets 1 pound boned
Large eggs 2, beaten
Butter 5½ tablespoons
Lemon juice from 1 lemon
Parsley 1 tablespoon minced

Mix bread crumbs and flour together and lightly salt and pepper fillets. Dip sole in beaten egg and roll in bread crumb mixture. Place fillets on waxed paper and allow breading to dry for 20 minutes. Heat frying pan and add 2½ tablespoons butter. Sauté sole over medium heat until golden brown. Turn only once. Remove fillets to preheated serving platter, and drain any remaining butter from pan. Heat remaining 3 tablespoons butter until lightly browned. Add lemon juice and parsley. Pour over fillets and serve immediately. Serves 4.
Variation: Oysters (16 ounces) done in this same manner are delicious.
Fish Substitutions:
    Pacific-Atlantic: snapper, sea bass
    Hawaiian: opakapaka, ono, shark (mako)

Snapper with Pesto Sauce

This is another of my family's favorites—but then, the Pesto Sauce complements any fish.

Pesto Sauce (see Index)   ½ cup
Flour   ¼ cup
Fine bread crumbs   ¾ cup
Salt and pepper   to taste
Snapper fillets   1½ pounds
Butter   3 tablespoons
Oil   1 tablespoon
Garlic clove   1, chopped
Lemon juice   from 1 lemon or
  Concentrated lemon juice   1 teaspoon
Dry white wine   ¼ cup

Make Pesto Sauce and set aside. Blend flour and bread crumbs. Salt and pepper fillets and roll in crumb mixture. Heat heavy skillet, preferably cast-iron, over medium-high heat. Add 2 tablespoons butter and 1 tablespoon oil. When heated, quickly sauté garlic. Add fillets and fry until golden, about 3 to 5 minutes. Turn and cook until underside is also golden. Remove to heated platter. Add 1 tablespoon butter to heated skillet, melt it, and add lemon juice and wine. Stir mixture well. Add sauce and heat through. Pour over fish and serve immediately. Serves 6.
Fish Substitutions:
  Pacific-Atlantic: lingcod, sole, turbot, codfish, sockeye salmon, halibut, bluefish
  Hawaiian: mahimahi, opakapaka, shark, sea bass

Fried Channel Catfish

Whenever I think of catfish, I have two visions that spring from my growing up next to the Mississippi River. One is of a small café called the Halfway Truck Stop, whose prime delicacy was a catfish sandwich—a favorite of both truckers and teen-agers. The other is of my family's landscaped fishpond, bordered by evergreens and filled with large, healthy gold and orange goldfish, and of my fishing father who loosed his catch of live channel catfish in the pond "just to keep 'em fresh," he said, until he was ready to cook them. Of course, the catfish had a royal feast at the expense of the goldfish. I can still hear my soft-spoken mother muttering in exasperated, hushed tones. Undoubtedly, she wanted to smack him with one of those ugly catfish, but instead, she cooked them. So, for memory's sake, here is the channel catfish prepared in the traditional southern method of my mother and her mother before her.

Channel catfish fillets   1½ pounds
Cornmeal   ½ cup
Salt   1 teaspoon
Shortening*   about ½-inch to 1-inch deep

Pat fillets dry. Blend cornmeal and salt and roll fillets in mixture. Heat heavy frying pan, preferably cast-iron, and add enough shortening to almost cover fillets. When shortening sizzles, about 375°, cook fillets 3 to 5 minutes per side, or until golden brown. Remove to heated platter and serve. Serves 4.
* If substituting a vegetable oil for the vegetable shortening, be aware that all vegetable oils are not suitable for deep frying. Check on yours before you use it.
Note: The best, simplest, and most traditional accompaniments for fried catfish are lemon wedges, Tartar Sauce (see Index), and hot cornbread.
Fish Substitutions:
Pacific-Atlantic: snapper, pike, turbot
Hawaiian: shark, ulua, ono, taape

Southern Deep-Fried Sauger

In a lake in Kentucky the sauger thrive, and my Uncle Jack has refined both his fishing and cooking skills to make the most of this fine-eating fish, which is similar to pike and which weighs in around 1½ to 3 pounds. With a propane gas tank hook-up to the burners, Jack is ready to entertain right at the dock beside his houseboat. Using a gallon of corn oil, he deep-fries the fish in a large, custom-made, cast-iron kettle. While Jack is tending the oil, Aunt Camille, who has an acclaimed magical hand in the kitchen, prepares the fish for frying and the rest of the meal—all with an eye for easily entertaining twenty people. And she does satisfy the crowds with this princely fish and its retinue—cheese grits, coleslaw, sliced tomatoes, hush puppies, and brownie cupcakes!

Sauger fillets   2 pounds
Buttermilk*   1 cup
Salt   to taste
Self-rising cornmeal   enough to roll fillets in or
   Corn muffin or cornbread ready-mix   8½-ounce box
Corn oil   to cover fillets
Lemon wedges   garnish

Dip fillets in buttermilk and roll in mixture of salt and cornmeal. Heat a heavy skillet, preferably cast-iron, and add oil. (If you're not using an electric skillet, use a thermometer to gauge correct heat.) When oil temperature reaches 370° to 375° (before smoking—smoking oil is too hot for frying fish), drop in fillets, being careful not to splatter, and cook until golden. When fillets are done, about 3 to 5 minutes, oil is ready for deep-fried accompaniments, such as hush puppies. Serves 4 to 6.
* Buttermilk gives a slightly sweet taste to the fish and enhances the natural flavor of the fillets.
Note: After the oil has cooled, strain it to remove any loose bits and store in refrigerator. You can even freeze it. With each use of the stored oil, always add some fresh oil to it.
Fish Substitutions:
   Pacific-Atlantic: halibut, sea bass, lingcod, scrod, bass, bluegill, crappie
   Hawaiian: opakapaka, mahimahi, rock cod

Shark Teriyaki

Soy sauce   2 tablespoons
Fresh ginger   1 small piece, crushed or
   Ground ginger   ¾ teaspoon
Mirin   2 teaspoons
Green onions   1 tablespoon chopped
Shark fillets or steaks   1 pound
Cornstarch   1 tablespoon
Light vegetable oil   3 tablespoons

Make marinade by combining soy sauce, ginger, mirin, and green onions. Marinate fish for 30 minutes or longer. Pat fish dry (reserving marinade) and roll in cornstarch, shaking excess. Heat skillet over medium-high heat. Add oil and heat again. Brown fillets quickly on both sides. Add reserved marinade and cook uncovered for 2 minutes or until fillets are done. Serves 4.

Note: I try to marinate the shark fillets or steaks for several hours, turning them occasionally; but even 30 minutes is sufficient. You may substitute the packaged dry mix of teriyaki marinade for the marinade given.

Fish Substitutions:
   Pacific-Atlantic: sea bass, lingcod, rockfish
   Hawaiian: butterfish, sea bass, taape

Black Cod Sukiyaki

This is a truly remarkable dish when you consider that one pound of fillets serves eight people. Because sukiyaki is always cooked at the last minute—indeed, in Japanese restaurants it is prepared in an electric skillet at your table—advance preparation is most essential! Be sure to allow yourself plenty of time for chopping ingredients and for assembling any other dishes you plan to serve. For example, prepare a salad (cucumber is good), make the soy plus wasabi paste dip, and prepare some fruit for dessert (melon or mandarin oranges are fitting); then turn your attention to the pièce de résistance—the sukiyaki.

Black cod fillets* 1 pound boned, cut in chunks
Soy sauce 1 cup
Sugar ¼ cup
Sake or mirin ¾ cup
Bean threads 4- or 5-ounce package
Light oil 2 tablespoons
Small onion 1, chopped
Bamboo shoots 8½-ounce can, drained, rinsed, and thinly sliced
Watercress small bunch, cut in 1-inch lengths
Green onion tops 3, cut in ½-inch lengths
Tofu 1 block, cubed
Soy sauce ½ cup (optional)
Wasabi paste ½ to 1 teaspoon (optional)
Egg 1, lightly beaten (optional)

Heat 1 cup soy sauce, sugar, and sake until sugar dissolves. (In microwave this takes 2 minutes at 100%; stir and cook 1 more minute at 100%.) Marinate fish chunks for one hour, turning only once. Steep bean threads in hot water for 3 minutes. Drain and cut into 4-inch lengths. (Or break before soaking.) Heat oil in a large skillet and sauté onion until translucent. Push to a corner of skillet, place fish cubes in skillet, and pour marinade over fish. Add bamboo shoot slices and watercress stems. Cook for 5 minutes over medium-high heat, stirring constantly. Add drained, cut bean threads and cook for another 3 minutes. (Use 2 spoons to stir the mixture if necessary.) Add green onion tops, watercress leaves, and tofu. Fold tofu in gently so it will not break. Stir sukiyaki gently until heated through. Serve immediately with soy sauce and wasabi paste (pour soy sauce in shallow dish and place wasabi on the side), or stir in a beaten raw egg just before serving. Serves 8.
* Bone fillets by placing them on a cutting board, noting the bone line running down the center of the fillets, and cutting down ⅛ inch on each side of that bone line. This should remove most bones, but for assurance, run your cleaned finger on each side where you just cut. You will be able

to feel any remaining bones, and if so, just cut them out.
Fish Substitutions:
   Pacific-Atlantic: rock cod, lingcod, sea trout, snapper
   Hawaiian: rock cod, shark (mako)

Shrimp Tempura

I can't think of shrimp tempura without picturing Sadame (pronounced Sa-da-may) Yamamoto standing in my kitchen in her white uniform, preparing her famous, mouth-watering specialty. I'm sorry to say this recipe is not Sadame's, but it is the closest I can come to duplicating it from knowledge and observation. Because most people are unfamiliar with tempura, I have divided the preparation into steps. I do prefer to use an electric skillet simply because I am better able to gauge the heat. While tempura is traditionally shrimp and vegetables, many fish such as lingcod, halibut, mahimahi, and shark may be served tempura-style. And remember, practice makes perfect!

Fresh shrimp   2 pounds, 16 to 20 per pound
Long eggplant   1, sliced (optional)
Green beans   8 ounces, trimmed (optional)
Lotus root   7-ounce can, sliced (optional)
Yam   1, peeled and sliced (optional)
Parsley   1 bunch (optional)
Tempura Sauce (see Index)   1¼ cups
Lemon wedges (optional)   garnish
Tempura Batter (see page 69)
Shortening   1 pound

Step 1:   Butterfly the shrimp.

Wash and shell shrimp, leaving on tails. Split shrimp down center of back to devein and rinse quickly in cold water. Now continue cutting through shrimp, going *almost*, but not quite, to other side. Flatten shrimp and turn over. Make 2 light diagonal slashes—just enough to prevent curling. Wrap shrimp and refrigerate. (If using shrimp smaller than 16 to 20 per pound, butterflying can be a tedious process. In that case, don't cut almost through to other side, but rather make slight slashes on the underside about every ½ inch.)

Step 2:   Prepare the vegetables.

Traditionally, several vegetables are served tempura-style with shrimp. These are done usually before you tempura shrimp, but it is not required. Some of the more preferable vegetables are sliced eggplant (long, skinny variety) which cannot be cut in advance because it will discolor, green beans, lotus root, sliced yams, and parsley. (Vegetables are more attractive if sliced diagonally.) Parsley is particularly difficult to do, and the secret is to shake off all excess batter before cooking. I prefer to thin the tempura batter for the vegetables. Make a thinner batter by taking 1 cup of the regular batter and adding 3 tablespoons of ice water to it. Stir only once and reserve this batter for vegetables. Put it on ice, naturally!

Step 3:   Make the Tempura Sauce for dipping.

Made with bonito flakes, this sauce is simple and complements tempura nicely. If you choose not to serve the Tempura Sauce, then serve the shrimp with lemon wedges.

Step 4:   Prepare the batter.

Prepare the batter according to the recipe provided. Meanwhile, of course, get your vegetables and shrimp ready to go.

Step 5:   Cook the tempura.

Heat shortening in electric frying pan, deep fryer, or cast-iron skillet until just *before* it smokes or to 370°. Melted shortening should be about 2 inches deep. Dip fingers into thinned batter and sprinkle over hot shortening. The result will be a thin, lacy batter forming on the top. Working quickly, do this 3 times. Now dip vegetables in thinned batter or shrimp in regular batter and proceed. Holding shrimp by tail, lay carefully on top of lacy batter. Do not crowd shrimp, or temperature of shortening will drop. Occasionally, you will need to skim surface of shortening to remove any loose bits of batter or food. Fry shrimp or vegetables until *barely* golden. Don't let them brown. Drain on paper towels and serve immediately with Tempura Sauce. Serves 6.

Tempura Batter

The Japanese do have a convenience product on the market called tempura batter, a dry mix to which you add water. I have not seen one yet, however, which tells you to use ice water, and I do remember that Sadame said the secret was to use ice water. Indeed, once she mixed the batter, she even set the bowl containing the batter into a larger bowl partially filled with ice water. The other secret to making a batter from scratch is to stir as little as possible.

Flour 1 cup
Cornstarch 1 cup
Large egg 1, beaten
Ice water 2 cups
Salt ½ teaspoon

Sift flour and cornstarch together in deep mixing bowl. Beat egg with whisk or chopsticks and add water, stirring constantly. Pour into dry mixture and stir, but don't overblend. (Chopsticks are excellent for stirring; they disturb less than a fork or spoon.) Place bowl containing batter in a larger bowl partially filled with ice water. (Now is the time to remove 1 cup of batter and add 3 tablespoons of ice water to it to form a thinner batter for vegetables.) Stir only once and place on ice. Makes 4 cups.

Snapper in Portuguese Vinha D'alhos

This recipe packs a dual formula for success—the Portuguese marinade and the panko flakes. It truly ranks among the top favorites with my family. My husband, the Virgo perfectionist, didn't even use a tartar sauce and returned surreptitiously to the pan and ate the remaining pieces.

Snapper fillets   1 pound
Portuguese Vinha D'alhos marinade*   1½-ounce package or
    Portuguese Marinade
Panko flakes   7-ounce package
Light oil   2 tablespoons
Lemon wedges   garnish
Tartar Sauce (see Index)   1¼ cups

Cut fillets crosswise so that pieces are about 2 inches by 4 inches by ½-inch or less. Marinate for 2 hours (longer if marinating in the homemade recipe), turning fillets after first hour. Spread some panko flakes on waxed paper and roll fish in it. Heat oil on medium-high. Fry fish until golden brown, turning once. (Time will depend upon thickness of fish; probably 6 to 8 minutes.) Serve immediately with lemon wedges and Tartar Sauce. Serves 4.

* I prefer to use the packaged dry mix called Portuguese Vinha D'alhos. If using this dry mix, turn your head when opening the package, for the powder is fine and strong. If you are unable to purchase the mix, try the substitute given below. It achieves a similar effect, but allow the flavors to blend for at least an hour before marinating the fish, and then marinate the fish for at least 4 hours.

Fish Substitutions:
    Pacific-Atlantic: sole, turbot, sea bass
    Hawaiian: rock cod, shark

Portuguese Marinade

Water   1 cup
Rice vinegar   ⅓ cup
Garlic cloves   2, minced
Ground cumin   ½ teaspoon
Salt   ¼ teaspoon
Powdered mustard   ½ teaspoon
Fine pepper   ⅛ teaspoon
Chili powder   ½ teaspoon
Dried red chili pepper   1 teaspoon crushed
Sugar   1½ teaspoons

Combine all ingredients and allow at least 1 hour to blend before marinating fish. Makes 1½ cups.

Lingcod Fish Fry

Some of my friends in Seattle related tales of catching lingcod instead of chinook or halibut. Disappointed, they gave it away. Forsooth! They could have had a grand party.

Lingcod 4 to 5 pounds, cut in 2-inch squares, ½-inch thick
Rock salt to taste
Honey ½ cup
Brandy ½ cup
Lemon peel 2 teaspoons grated or
  Ground lemon peel 2 teaspoons
Flour 3 cups
Light beer 1½ pints
Shortening enough to form 2-inch depth in pan

Cut cod into 2-inch squares, ½-inch thick, and place in a 9 by 13-inch shallow glass dish. Sprinkle liberally with rock salt. Mix honey, brandy, and lemon peel and pour over fish. Marinate for at least 2 hours, turning fish after first hour. Blend flour and beer to form a smooth batter. In a large frying pan heat shortening to 375°. (Don't permit shortening to smoke.) Without drying, dip squares of fish in batter and fry until golden. When one side is golden, promptly turn it over. When both sides have lightly browned, remove immediately. Do not overcook. Serve very hot. Serves 12.
Note: If you have leftovers, wrap carefully after cooling and seal in freezer bags. When you desire to use them, thaw, place on a brown paper bag on a cookie sheet in a preheated 400° oven, and reheat for 10 to 15 minutes.
Fish Substitutions:
  Pacific-Atlantic: codfish, halibut, bluefish
  Hawaiian: mahimahi, shark (mako)

Stamp 'n' Go Rock Cod Sandwiches

This is a variation of the popular sandwich in Jamaica, and it can be a refreshing departure from hamburgers. I use a food processor to chop and blend the ingredients, but nimble fingers can do the same. Remember to prepare the accompaniments before cooking the sandwiches—slice the tomatoes, break the lettuce, butter the buns and place them on a broiler rack.

Rock cod fillets   ¾ pound, finely chopped
Large scallion   1, including top, chopped
Parsley   2 tablespoons chopped
White pepper   ⅛ teaspoon
Salt   ¼ teaspoon
Dried red chili pepper   ¼ teaspoon crushed
Lime juice   1 teaspoon
Milk   1 tablespoon
Flour   1 tablespoon
Bacon grease   1 tablespoon or
    Butter   1 tablespoon, softened
Egg   1
Double-action baking powder   ⅛ teaspoon
Flour   ⅓ cup
Bread crumbs   ⅓ cup
Eggs   2, beaten
Light vegetable oil   1 tablespoon
Butter   2 tablespoons
Large buns   5, preferably onion
Tartar Sauce (see Index)   1¼ cups
Lettuce   garnish
Tomato slices   garnish
Lemon wedges   garnish
Parsley   garnish

Chop and blend first 12 ingredients. Chill mixture for at least 1 hour. Dipping hands in flour, shape fish mixture into patties. Mix ⅓ cup flour and bread crumbs. Dip each patty in beaten eggs, then roll in bread crumb mixture. Preheat frying pan to medium-high. Add oil and butter, reduce heat to medium, and fry patties until golden on both sides. Meanwhile, toast buns under broiler. Serve sandwiches open-face with Tartar Sauce, lettuce, and a tomato slice on the side. Garnish with lemon wedges and parsley. Serves 5.

Fish Substitutions:
    Pacific-Atlantic: salmon, snapper, codfish, scrod
    Hawaiian: shark (mako), weke-ula, taape

Basque Scrambled Eggs with Crab

This is one of my favorite meals for stretching the budget. Buy a small crab or canned crab when it's on sale and watch it serve four. Crusty French bread and potatoes are the perfect complement to this!

Vegetable oil   2 tablespoons
Large onion   1, diced
Parsley-Garlic Mix (see Index)   2 teaspoons
Small green pepper   1, seeded and diced
Small sweet red pepper   1, seeded and diced or
   Large pimiento   1, diced
Large tomato*   1, peeled, seeded, and chopped
Tabasco   3 to 6 drops, depending upon taste
Salt and pepper   to taste
Small fresh crab   1 cleaned or
   Canned crab   6-ounce can
Eggs   6, beaten
Heavy cream   ¼ cup
Butter   2 tablespoons

Heat a heavy frying pan, preferably cast-iron. Add oil and heat over medium-high. Sauté onions and Parsley-Garlic Mix for 15 seconds. Immediately add next 6 ingredients. Stir gently, but thoroughly. Reduce heat to low and simmer uncovered for about 8 minutes, stirring frequently. Add crab and heat through. Set aside, keeping warm. Beat eggs with cream. Heat another large frying pan and melt butter over medium to medium-high heat. Add egg mixture and stir constantly. When eggs are still very soft and shiny, fold in crab mixture. Serve immediately. Serves 4.
* To peel the tomato, dip it in boiling water, then quickly immerse it in cold water; the skin can then be easily removed. Of course, our friend Lou, who has a gas stove, simply jabs the tomato with a fork, turns a burner on medium, and quickly twirls the tomato *over*, not in, the flame. The skin peels with ease.

Sockeye Newburg

Sockeye salmon steaks   6
Salt and white pepper   to taste
Flour   enough to dust lightly
Butter   ¼ cup
Newburg Sauce (see Index)   1½ cups
Parsley   garnish

Sprinkle steaks with salt and pepper and dredge in flour. Heat butter in large frying pan, preferably cast-iron. Fry steaks over medium to medium-high heat for about 4 minutes on one side; turn and cook underside until cooked through. Transfer steaks to a heated serving platter or warmed dinner plates. Spoon ¼ cup hot sauce over each steak and serve immediately. Garnish with parsley. Serves 6.
Variations: Crab may be substituted for the sockeye if you prefer. Simply add the cleaned crab meat to the sauce while heating it over the double boiler and serve over toast or English muffins. Also, you may easily substitute a hollandaise or other sauce for the Newburg.
Fish Substitutions:
    Pacific-Atlantic: halibut, sturgeon, crab
    Hawaiian: opakapaka, onaga, mahimahi

Marinated Eel

No seafood cookbook would be complete without an eel recipe. (Although I don't know why I say that since I haven't included recipes for the manta ray or the nautilus.) If you feel you must try eel—and some people, you know, do believe they must sample a little bit of everything—try the white eel.

Lemon juice ¼ cup
Light vegetable oil ⅛ cup
Garlic clove 1, minced
Salt ½ teaspoon
White pepper ¼ teaspoon
Dry white wine 2 tablespoons
Onion 1 tablespoon minced
Parsley 1 tablespoon chopped
Small red chili pepper 1, seeded and diced
Small white eel* 1, cleaned and boned or cut in sections

Combine first 9 ingredients and add eel. Soak overnight. Sauté eel in frying pan over medium-high heat in oil until done. Serves 4.

* Skinning the eel can be done 1 of 2 ways. The first method is to slit the neck all the way around, being certain to cut through the skin. Tie a rope or twine around its neck above the slit and secure the rope to a nail in your rafter. Using pliers, seize the skin at the slit and pull downward. Continue this process until eel is peeled.

The second and more time-consuming method is to cut the eel into 2- to 3-inch sections with a cleaver. In a large pot of simmering water repeatedly dip the eel sections until the skin loosens. Remove the eel and scrape away the skin. In another pot, add ½ cup salt to a quart of water and soak the scraped eel for 15 minutes.

Note: It is important to soak the eel overnight in the marinade; eel can have a strong taste and the marinade cuts that plus tenderizes the meat. There still remains the problem of bones. Because I do have young children, I try to remove the bones before I cook, so with eel I bone it before I even marinate it. However, it might be easier to bone it after cooking.

Snapper à la King for Two

Butter   2 tablespoons
Onion   1 tablespoon chopped
Green pepper   1 tablespoon chopped
Mushrooms   ¼ cup sliced
Snapper fillets   ½ pound
Condensed cream of celery soup   10¾-ounce can
Lemon juice   1½ teaspoons
Cayenne   dash
Salt and pepper   to taste
Sherry   1½ teaspoons
Pimiento   1½ tablespoons, minced
Toast, muffins, egg noodles, or rice

Melt butter in frying pan and sauté onion, green pepper, mushrooms, and snapper until tender. Stir in remaining ingredients (except toast) and heat thoroughly over medium heat, stirring frequently. Serve over toast, muffins, egg noodles, or rice. Serves 2.
Fish Substitutions:
    Pacific-Atlantic: flounder, turbot
    Hawaiian: weke, taape

Broiled
and
Barbecued

Barbecued Whole Salmon

Olive Brown has a knack with a fishing pole, and she loves to land the salmon. While her guests rave about her barbecued salmon, Olive honestly prefers the leftovers the following day in Creamed Salmon.

Salmon*   one 4- to 5-pound before dressing, or 3- to 4-pound dressed
Celery salt   to taste
Pepper   to taste
Dill weed   1 teaspoon minced
Scallions   3, chopped, including tops
Lemon slices   6
Small celery tops   2, including leaves
Dry white wine   ½ cup
Butter   3 tablespoons
Lemon slices   garnish
Paprika   garnish
Parsley   garnish
Pimiento-stuffed green olive   garnish

Quickly rinse fish, pat dry, and place on heavy-duty foil. Sprinkle cavity with celery salt, pepper, dill weed, and scallions. Arrange 6 lemon slices and celery tops in cavity. Pour ¼ cup wine in cavity and dot with 1½ tablespoons butter. Pour remaining wine on top of fish and dot with remaining butter. Arrange 5 lemon slices sprinkled with paprika over body of fish and sprinkle parsley over fish. Close foil loosely and cook over hot coals for 15 to 20 minutes. Open foil and cook for another 5 to 10 minutes. Place slices of stuffed green olive over the eye and serve immediately. Serves 6.
* Since the heat of the coals varies, allow 5 to 10 extra minutes accordingly. If cooking a large fish and the coals aren't quite hot enough, pop the fish under the broiler for a few minutes before serving.
Note: Hostess Potatoes (see Index) and broccoli are excellent companions to the barbecued salmon.
Fish Substitutions:
   Pacific-Atlantic: bluefish, snapper, pike
   Hawaiian: opakapaka, kumu, uku, weke-ula, muu

Broiled Salmon Diable

This is an easy and different way of preparing salmon. A cucumber salad is the perfect counterpoint to this devilishly good dish!

Salmon 2 pounds unskinned
Salt and pepper to taste
Escoffier Diable Sauce or Pickapeppa Sauce ½ cup
Butter ¼ cup, melted
Dry white wine ½ cup
Parsley 1 teaspoon minced
Parsley garnish
Lemon slices garnish
Cucumber slices garnish

Line a broiler pan with foil and place slabs of salmon on foil. Preheat broiler and place rack about 6 inches from heating element. Lightly salt and pepper fish. Stir together sauce, butter, wine, and parsley. Score fish diagonally every 2 inches. Baste fish well with mixture. Broil approximately 20 minutes, depending upon thickness of slabs. (Allow 10 minutes for every inch.) Baste several times while cooking. Garnish with clumps of parsley, lemon slices, and cucumber. Serves 6 to 8.
Fish Substitutions:
    Pacific-Atlantic: halibut, mackerel, pompano
    Hawaiian: mahimahi, papio, ulua

Opakapaka Slow Cook

This refreshing barbecue is akin to the Oven-Steamed Kumu except that it requires a split fish cooked on the barbecue. A split fish, by the way, is one that has been scaled, cleaned, and has had the head, tail, fins, and backbone removed. The fish is then split open into two long halves. They are cooked skin side down and are not turned during cooking.

Opakapaka   one 2½-pound dressed and split
Salt and white pepper   to taste
Butter-Wine Sauce (see Index)   ¾ cup
Small onion   1, thinly sliced
Lemon   1, thinly sliced
Parsley   1 tablespoon minced
Capers   2 tablespoons
Onion slices   garnish
Lemon slices   garnish
Parsley   garnish

Prepare barbecue, setting coals as far away from grill as possible. Lightly grease a foil boat and place fish halves on it skin side down. Lightly salt and pepper fish. Heat sauce and pour half over fish. Arrange sliced onion and lemon over fish halves. Sprinkle parsley and capers over lemon and onion. When coals have peaked and are beginning to ebb, place foil boat on grill. Cover, preferably with a barbecue lid. (If barbecue does not have a lid, use foil and crimp edges around lip of foil boat.) Allow about 10 minutes per pound depending upon heat of coals. Halfway through cooking time, baste fish with remaining sauce. Do not turn fish. To test for doneness, insert toothpick in thickest part of fish. The toothpick should meet minimum resistance and meat should have lost translucence. To serve, gently slide fish halves onto preheated serving platter. Garnish with onion, lemon slices, and clumps of green parsley. Serves 4.

Fish Substitutions:
    Pacific-Atlantic: salmon, pike, halibut
    Hawaiian: mahimahi, uku, weke-ulu, muu

Parrot Fish with Sausage

Parrot fish is known for its splendid bright colors and strong taste. Here the sausage balances the flavor, and the foil keeps the fish steamy moist.

Parrot fish   one 3-pound dressed and split
Salt and pepper   to taste
Mayonnaise   3 to 4 tablespoons
Ring sausage*   10 to 12 slices or more, depending upon diameter of
    sausage

Prepare barbecue coals. Lightly grease a foil boat and place fish halves on it skin side down. Salt and pepper fish. Spread mayonnaise over halves and arrange sausage slices. Close foil tightly and barbecue until translucence is gone, about 40 to 50 minutes. Serves 6.
* The Chinese-style sausage known as *lup chong* is good, as are Portuguese and Polish sausages.

Ono Teriyaki BBQ*

Ono   one 1½- to 2-pound dressed and split
Salt and white pepper   to taste
Soy sauce   ¼ cup
Fresh ginger   1 small piece, crushed or
    Ground ginger   1 teaspoon
Mirin   1 tablespoon plus 1 teaspoon
Green onions   2 tablespoons chopped

Prepare barbecue coals. Lightly grease a foil boat and set fish halves on it skin side down. Salt and pepper fish. Score fish diagonally every 2 inches. Mix soy sauce, ginger, mirin, and green onions together. Pour over fish, making certain that mixture flows into scoring. Close foil tightly. Allow 25 to 40 minutes, depending upon heat of coals, until fish loses translucence in thickest part. Serves 3 to 4.
* Packaged or bottled teriyaki sauce may be substituted for the teriyaki mixture in this recipe.
Fish Substitutions:
    Pacific-Atlantic: salmon, pike, bass, lingcod, bluefish, black cod
    Hawaiian: uku, weke-ula, muu, parrot fish

Grilled Sturgeon with Mushroom Sauce

Sturgeon is my most favorite fish of all. Prehistoric, it has a grotesque appearance by the standards of any trout lover. But don't be deceived by appearances, for underneath the tough skin and bony plates lie tender morsels of meat fit only for gods. Sturgeon has a distinctively rich flavor and firm texture—some compare it with veal. The problem is that it is either so scarce or unknown that few restaurants offer it. Fortunately, however, it may occasionally be found in the fish markets, and if it is, get it!

Packaged mushroom sauce or Knorr-Swiss Hunter Sauce*   1 cup
Cognac   1 teaspoon (optional)
Mushrooms   2 large or 3 medium
Butter   6 tablespoons
Sturgeon steaks   four, ¾- to 1-inch thick
Salt and white pepper   to taste
Parsley   2 tablespoons minced
Lemon wedges   garnish

Prepare packaged sauce mix, adding cognac if desired, and set aside. Gently rinse mushrooms, blot dry, and thinly slice. Sauté mushrooms in 2 tablespoons butter, drain with slotted spoon, and add to sauce, stirring gently. Preheat broiler to maximum heat. Grease heavy-duty foil, crimping edges to form a shallow pan. Place steaks on foil, season with salt and pepper, and dot with 2 tablespoons butter. Place foil on broiler rack about 6 inches from heating element and close oven door. Broil for 3 minutes. Baste steaks with juices and broil for another 2 minutes. With spatula carefully turn over steaks and dot with remaining 2 tablespoons butter. Put sauce on simmer to begin reheating. Close oven and broil steaks for 3 minutes. Baste and broil for another 2 to 3 minutes. Test for doneness by piercing with fork near center. (Fork should meet with minimum resistance and meat should have lost translucence.) Allowing ¼ cup sauce per steak, pour sauce over steaks. Sprinkle with parsley and serve with lemon wedge. Serves 4.
* I usually use the packaged Knorr-Swiss Mushroom Sauce. However, you certainly may use any package of regular brown gravy mix (in which case the cognac is highly recommended) or, naturally, a cup of homemade sauce would be welcomed.
Fish Substitutions:
    Pacific-Atlantic: halibut, pompano
    Hawaiian: mahimahi, bluerunner, papio, ulua

Polynesian Steelhead BBQ

Tom Reaves lives in Anchorage, Alaska, and operates the Little Fisherman Seafood Shoppe. He is a fisherman extraordinaire and an even better storyteller—if that's possible. To boot, he's a good cook, and he knows how to prepare his catch. Below are his special marinade and method for preparing his steelhead. Long beans and country-fried potatoes add to this great barbecue treat!

Spañada 1 cup
Honey ½ cup
Soy sauce 1 cup
Garlic cloves 5, crushed
Fresh ginger ⅓ inch, sliced and crushed or
    Ground ginger ½ teaspoon
Steelhead steaks 6, about ¾- to 1-inch thick
Salt and white pepper to taste
Pineapple or papaya ½ cup crushed

Pour Spañada in saucepan and add honey, soy sauce, garlic, and ginger. Heat until honey dissolves. Cool. Place steaks in 8-inch square glass baking dish and sprinkle with salt and pepper. Add fruit to marinade and pour over steaks. Marinate for at least 1 hour (the longer the better, even overnight), turning steaks twice. Get charcoal hot and oil grate so fish will not stick. Barbecue over medium heat 7 minutes on each side. During this time, turn steaks twice, basting each time. Serves 6.
Fish Substitutions:
    Pacific-Atlantic: salmon, halibut, bonita, albacore
    Hawaiian: mahimahi, bluerunner, ulua

Broiled Halibut with Anchovy Butter

Butter   2 tablespoons, room temperature
Anchovy paste   1 teaspoon
Cayenne   ⅛ teaspoon
Salt   ¼ teaspoon
Halibut steaks   2
Lemon wedges   garnish
Parsley   garnish

Preheat broiler to maximum heat. Grease foil to prevent fish from sticking; make a little boat of foil. Cream butter with anchovy paste. Add cayenne and salt and mix well. Lightly spread ½ mixture over steaks. Place steaks in foil under broiler for about 4 minutes. Turn steaks and baste with juices, and broil for another 4 minutes. Melt remaining anchovy butter until slightly browned (but don't let it burn). Serve steaks with browned butter and juices poured over steaks or serve butter and juices in small bowl for dipping. Garnish with lemon wedges and minced parsley. Serves 2.
Fish Substitutions:
  Pacific-Atlantic: salmon, pompano
  Hawaiian: mahimahi, shark, papio

Scallops Yakitori

Yakitori in Japanese means "to broil over charcoal," and Japanese restaurants with yakiniku *in their names offer barbecues over a gas grill. Each table has its own hibachi where guests broil and baste their own assortments of meats and vegetables. One might say it is the Japanese version of shish kabob, only thin bamboo skewers are used to hold the meats and vegetables. If you have a small hibachi, set out a plate of scallops and vegetables, such as green peppers, tomatoes, onions, and mushrooms, and let your guests make their own.*

Sugar   2 tablespoons
Soy sauce   3 tablespoons
Sake   ¼ cup
Scallops   2 pounds (if very large, cut in smaller chunks)
Pineapple   1, cored and cut into 1 by 2-inch rectangles or
  Assorted vegetables   (cherry tomatoes, green peppers, onions)

Heat sugar, soy sauce, and sake until sugar dissolves. Place scallops in deep glass bowl and cover with sauce. Chill in refrigerator for at least 1 hour, preferably longer. Core and prepare pineapple or arrange plate of assorted vegetables. Get charcoal hot and oil grate if barbecuing; otherwise, preheat broiler. Alternate scallops with pineapple cubes (or vegetables) on bamboo skewers. Baste with sauce before cooking. Turn scallops frequently, basting each turn. Cook until tender, about 5 to 7 minutes, depending upon heat. Serve immediately. Serves 6.

Variation: If you don't wish to make your own sauce, you may always use the packaged teriyaki mix—just add a splash of sake to it.

Note: Serve with rice and a tomato-green pepper salad. If serving on a tray, place the pineapple top as a centerpiece in the tray and arrange the skewers around it. (If using the vegetables, then substitute a fruit salad for the vegetable one.) And remember, if you are serving sake as a beverage, it should be warmed.

Fish Substitutions:
Pacific-Atlantic: salmon, shrimp, halibut
Hawaiian: mahimahi, shrimp

Broiled Ulua Pickapeppa Steaks

Ulua steaks   4
Salt and white pepper   to taste
Pickapeppa Sauce   enough to spread
Parsley   garnish
Lemon wedges   garnish

Preheat broiler to maximum and grease a small boat of foil. Place steaks on foil and lightly salt and pepper them. Spread Pickapeppa Sauce on steaks, about a teaspoon each. Place steaks under broiler about 6 inches from heating element and close oven door. Broil for about 4 minutes or less, depending upon thickness of steaks. Baste with juices in foil and turn; spread more sauce, and broil for another 2 minutes. Garnish with minced parsley and serve with lemon wedges. Serves 4.

Fish Substitutions:
Pacific-Atlantic: mackerel, pompano, halibut
Hawaiian: papio, mahimahi

Fresh Maine Lobster with Tarragon Butter Sauce

Maine lobster is renowned everywhere—even in France. The Zanes discovered this version with its mouth-watering sauce in a small French inn. Sheldon says it's really "Homard grillé au beurre d'estragon." I'll take his word for it!

Fresh Maine lobsters   two 1½- to 1½-pound each
Olive oil   to baste
Shallots   2 tablespoons minced
Unsalted butter   1 cup
Dried tarragon leaves   2 teaspoons crumbled
Lobster coral (roe)   from lobsters, diced
Tomatoes   garnish
Cucumbers   garnish
Pimientos   garnish
Scrambled eggs   garnish

Split live lobster lengthwise and clean, saving the coral (the roe). Crack claws with nutcracker and pour oil over meat and shell. Broil 6 to 7 inches from broiler element at 485° for 12 minutes. After 6 minutes, baste with more oil. Make sauce by sautéing shallots in melted butter. Add tarragon and lobster coral and simmer for 4 minutes. Pour over lobster and broil for additional 1 to 2 minutes. Garnish lobster cavity with diced tomatoes, cucumbers, pimientos, or scrambled eggs. Serve warm. Serves 2.

Favorite Specialties

Island Curry

When I make Island Curry, I like to sing along with a Broadway musical. While a song from The King and I *would be more appropriate, I usually find myself singing a tune from the heartland, such as "People Will Say We're in Love." As the crescendo builds, I sing louder and stir harder. The neighbors love it and say, "The Wrights are having fish again—we can* hear *it!"*

Sea bass* 1 pound, cut in bite-sized chunks
Marinade 1:
    Coconut milk half 12-ounce can
    Fresh or bottled lime juice 1 tablespoon
    Red chili pepper ¼ teaspoon finely minced
Marinade 2:
    Pineapple juice from 1 whole fruit
    Pineapple spears enough to lay on top of fish
Marinade 3:
    Fresh or bottled lemon juice ½ cup
    Fresh or bottled lime juice ¼ cup
    Red chili pepper ¼ teaspoon finely minced
Curry seasonings:
    Turmeric 1 teaspoon
    Ground cumin ¾ teaspoon
    Dijon mustard ½ teaspoon
    Salt ½ teaspoon
    Red chili pepper ¾ teaspoon finely minced
Butter 3 tablespoons
Garlic cloves 2, pressed
Small onion 1, diced
Velouté Sauce (see Index) 1½ cups
Rice

Choose 1 of the 3 marinades, mix ingredients for it, and marinate fish in glass bowl for at least 1 hour. Cover and place dish in refrigerator, turning fish occasionally. Make the curry seasonings by mixing spices noted. In large frying pan or Dutch oven, melt butter over medium heat. When bubbling, add garlic, onion, and curry seasonings. Stir constantly while sautéing onions until just translucent. Add sauce and stir until heated through. Add fish chunks and stir constantly over medium-high heat until fish is just cooked through (just a few minutes to lose translucence). Do not overcook! Serve over rice. Serves 3 to 4.
* Shark (mako) does very nicely in curry; however, it does become flaky around the edges and thus does not give as nice an apperance as other

firm-fleshed fish.

Note: Since coconut milk (available in the frozen foods section) or fresh pineapple is not always carried in markets, I have provided 3 different marinades for the fish. Each will give a slightly different taste, but all blend well with the curry seasonings.

Fish Substitutions:

Pacific-Atlantic: halibut, haddock, bluefish, snapper

Hawaiian: shark (mako), ono, muu, uku

Creamed Finnan Haddie

White Sauce (see Index)*   2 cups
Finnan haddie   ¾ pound
Lemon juice   2 tablespoons
Cayenne   ⅛ teaspoon
Watercress   1 tablespoon minced
Toast   4 slices
Lemon wedges   garnish
Dilled potatoes

Make White Sauce in double boiler and set aside. Cut finnan haddie into cubes and gently stir into sauce along with lemon juice and cayenne. Cover and heat over, but not in, boiling water for 20 to 25 minutes, stirring occasionally. Garnish with watercress. Serve on toast with lemon wedges and dilled potatoes. Serves 4.

* The packaged mix for white sauce works just fine. Since finnan haddie is smoked haddock or cod, it has ample salt content, so *do not* add salt to the sauce.

Fish Substitutions:

Pacific-Atlantic: salmon (poached), sea bass (poached)

Hawaiian: opakapaka, uku, ono, weke-ula, papio, akule

Creamed Salmon

The day Olive Brown prepares her barbecued salmon, she also prepares the frozen patty shells for the creamed salmon. She does not refrigerate them after she bakes them, but rather places them in a snug plastic bag when they cool. The following day, she prepares her creamed salmon and pours it over the patty shells. This makes a nice brunch and lends itself to a chafing dish. Serve with chilled melons.

White Sauce (see Index)   2 cups
Dry white wine   2 tablespoons
Green onions   1½, chopped, including tops
Eggs   2, hard-cooked and minced
Salt and pepper   to taste
Salmon   1¾ cups cooked
Frozen patty shells   4, baked
Parsley   garnish

Make sauce and add next 5 ingredients. Add salmon and heat through. Serve on patty shells and garnish with minced parsley. Serves 4 to 5.

Scampi with Fettucine

There is always a special ambience about my mother-in-law's dinners—a beautiful table, an exquisite garden setting framed in spotlights, and lit candles. Curiously, while everyone raves about her cooking, she maintains that she does only the simplest of dinners. Here is one of her favorites which she serves with a green salad followed by a dessert of ice cream with berries.

Butter   2 tablespoons plus 1 teaspoon
Garlic cloves   4, minced or pressed
Shrimp   2 pounds, shelled and deveined
Scallion   1, finely sliced
White wine   dash
Salt   to taste
Fettucine noodles   ½ to 1 pound
Pesto Sauce (see Index)*   1 cup
Parsley   garnish

Warm dinner plates in the oven. Cook noodles in boiling water, unless using fresh. Heat large skillet, preferably cast-iron, and melt butter. Add garlic and stir just until beginning to turn golden. Add shrimp and scallion and stir gently until shrimp just turn pink, about 2 to 3 minutes. Do not overcook! Sprinkle wine over scampi, salt, and stir for 1 minute. Meanwhile, drain noodles and toss with heated Pesto Sauce until coated. Place a portion of scampi and fettucine on plates, sprinkle with parsley, and serve immediately. Serves 6.

* This particular pesto may be too strong for the delicate scampi. You may wish to use a frozen pesto sauce (sold in specialty food shops and in the frozen food sections of some groceries) or perhaps serve Fettucine Alfredo instead.

Note: To save time, make Pesto Sauce a day or so before the meal, shell shrimp early in day and refrigerate in plastic sack, and prepare green salad (except for adding tomatoes and dressing).

If using fresh noodles, allow only 30 seconds to 1 minute cooking time. Also, sauce seems to adhere better to the imported Italian fettucce or the spiral noodle.

Crab with Mousseline Sauce in Ramekins

This is an absolutely delightful first course, brunch, or light supper. You can prepare the ramekins in advance up to the point of adding the toasted bread crumbs; however, since refrigerated ramekins will require slightly longer time under the broiler, be sure the crumbs are not too toasted. The Mousseline Sauce is simply superb!

Fresh crab meat   3 cups (about 2 Dungeness crabs)
Pimientos   2 tablespoons chopped
Mayonnaise   6 tablespoons
Salt and white pepper   to taste
Chives   1 tablespoon chopped
Shallots   1 tablespoon diced
Nutmeg   dash
Mousseline Sauce (see Index)   1 cup
Fine bread crumbs   3 tablespoons, lightly toasted

Mix all ingredients, except sauce and bread crumbs, and place in 6 individual ramekins or scallop shells. Make sauce and pour over crab. Top with bread crumbs, about 1½ teaspoons per ramekin. If not refrigerated, broil about 5 inches from heating element until glazed. If it has been refrigerated, broil about 7 inches from heating element for about 4 minutes. Serves 6.

Shrimp Coquilles with Mousseline Sauce

This is another variation of the crab ramekins, except that it is made with shrimp. Like the crab, this makes an excellent first course, but I also serve it as a brunch.

Shrimp*   3 cups cooked, shelled, and deveined
Pimientos   2 tablespoons chopped
Mayonnaise   6 tablespoons
Salt and white pepper   to taste
Chives   1 tablespoon chopped
Shallots   1 tablespoon diced
Nutmeg   dash
Mousseline Sauce (see Index)   1 cup
Fine bread crumbs   3 tablespoons, lightly toasted

Mix all ingredients, except sauce and bread crumbs, and place in 6 individual scallop shells. Make sauce and pour over shrimp. Top with bread crumbs, about 1½ teaspoons per shell. If not refrigerated, broil about 5 inches from heating element until glazed. If refrigerated, broil about 7 inches from heating element for about 4 minutes. Serves 6.

* Cook the shrimp in a Court-Bouillon (see Index), and please, do not overcook them. Since you will be reheating them, take them from the hot water as soon as they turn pink. For 6 people, you will need about 2 pounds of unshelled shrimp (50 to 60 per pound). I prefer this size, because anything larger overwhelms the scallop shells, but you could use the smaller tiny bay shrimp.

Linguine with White Clam Sauce*

My Irish party friend, Joan, pays tribute to the Italians with her simple version of this linguine with white clam sauce. Served on a silver tray it is truly an elegant meal, totally disguising its bargain price tag. And to heighten the elegance, you can use fresh clams and even add steamed-open clams in the shell as a decorative border for the tray. Serve with crusty French bread, softened butter, and an emerald spinach salad and your guests will be delighted.

Linguine   1 pound, cooked and drained
Chicken bouillon   3 cubes, dissolved in hot water (according to
    package directions)
Clam juice   reserved from canned clams, about 1⅓ cups
Butter   ½ cup
Parsley-Garlic Mix (see Index)   2 tablespoons
Arrowroot   2 tablespoons dissolved in small amount of cold water or
    Cornstarch   1 tablespoon dissolved in small amount of cold water
Minced clams   three 20-ounce cans, drained, juice reserved
Grated Romano cheese   garnish

Begin cooking linguine before starting sauce if linguine is packaged, dry variety. (If fresh, place in boiling water about 1 minute before sauce is completed.) Mix bouillon and clam juice (total should be about 2 cups). Melt butter in large frying pan, add Parsley-Garlic Mix, and sauté over medium heat for 1 minute. Pour in liquid, add arrowroot, and simmer uncovered for 8 minutes. Add drained clams and warm through. Pour sauce over drained, hot linguine and serve with grated cheese. Serves 8.
* To serve family-style, place linguine on a large oval platter and pour hot clam sauce over it. To serve as appetizers, place a helping of cooked linguine in individual ovenproof seashells or ramekins, top with a serving of clam sauce, and sprinkle grated Romano over the tops. Cover and refrigerate until ready to cook. Reheat uncovered in a preheated 400° oven for 10 to 15 minutes. This will make 12 to 14 individual appetizers. (Remember, since arrowroot will not hold in reheating, use cornstarch to thicken the sauce if you do plan to reheat.)

Calamari

Fried squid, or calamari, is becoming increasingly popular and is even gaining a reputation as the "poor man's abalone." While the mantle can be served whole and stuffed, I prefer to cut it into rings. It goes further, works as a great appetizer, and when I know people well, I serve it for dinner with a cold, cooked Italian salad made of broccoli, cauliflower, artichoke hearts, cherry tomatoes, and seasonings.

Squid* 1 pound, cleaned
Panko flakes 4-ounce package or
    Fine bread crumbs ¾ cup
Parmesan cheese 2 tablespoons
Eggs 2, beaten
Garlic salt to taste
Butter 2 tablespoons
Oil 2 tablespoons

Cut hoods into rings approximately ¼-inch wide; leave smaller tentacles whole. Toss panko flakes with cheese and spread on waxed paper. Dip rings and tentacles in egg and roll in panko mixture. Sprinkle with garlic salt. Preheat skillet, preferably cast-iron. When heated, add butter and oil. Fry rings and tentacles at medium-high until golden and done, about 10 minutes. Drain on paper towels and serve immediately. Serves 4.
* See Index for instructions on cleaning squid.

Gravlax—Salmon Marinated in Dill

My Swedish friend, Kris, introduced me to this marvelous Scandinavian cured dish. It is pronounced "grahve-lox." She serves this as an appetizer or as a light supper; it also makes an unusual brunch.

Salmon 1 center-cut portion 3 to 3½ pounds, cleaned and scaled
Fresh dill 1 large bunch
Rock salt ¼ cup
Sugar ¼ cup
White peppercorns 2 tablespoons crushed
Lemon wedges garnish
Parsley garnish
Toast 8 to 10 slices
Gravlaxsås

Cut salmon in half lengthwise and bone. Place fish, skin side down, in a deep 9 by 13-inch glass dish. Arrange dill on fish. Combine salt, sugar, and crushed peppercorns and sprinkle over fish. Top with other ½ fish, skin side up, and cover with foil. Set a heavy platter or plate on fish. Pile weights on top of platter, such as 3 or 4 cans of food. (The important point is to weight fish as evenly as possible.) Refrigerate for 48 hours (or up to 3 days). Every 12 hours, separate halves and baste with liquid. Then replace top ½ and turn fish over. When gravlax is finished, remove from marinade. Scrape away dill and seasonings. Pat dry with paper towels. Place fish halves, skin side down, on a carving board. Slice salmon thinly, on diagonal, detaching each slice from skin. Garnish with lemon wedges and clumps of parsley. Serve with toast and Gravlaxsås. Serves 8 to 10.

Fish Substitutions:
  Pacific-Atlantic: steelhead
  Hawaiian: onaga, ahi

Gravlaxsås (Mustard and Dill Sauce)

Dijon mustard* ¼ cup
Dry mustard 1 teaspoon
Sugar 3 tablespoons
Vinegar 2 tablespoons (raspberry or white)
Vegetable oil ⅓ cup
Fresh dill 3 tablespoons chopped or
  Dried dill 1 teaspoon

In a small deep bowl mix the 2 mustards, sugar, and vinegar to a paste. With wire whisk slowly beat in oil until a thick mayonnaise-like emulsion forms. Blend in chopped dill. Sauce may be refrigerated in a tightly-covered jar for several days. However, before serving again, shake jar vigorously or beat sauce with whisk to reblend ingredients. Makes ¾ cup.
* This mustard should be a dark, highly seasoned variety, such as Dijon Grained Mustard with Burgundy Wine by Maitre Jacques.

St. Charles's Paella for Twenty

Charles Izumoto, Jr., earned the title of saint before his name because he performs miracles in his kitchen. Unhesitatingly, he gave me his private recipe for paella for twenty. He laughingly said that this is not a true paella because he omits the chicken. Believe me—nobody misses it! Serve buffet-style with hot, buttered French bread and a tossed green salad.

Step 1:   Prepare the seasonings and vegetables.

Garlic clove   1, minced
Onions   2, minced
Large red bell pepper   1, minced
Frozen artichoke hearts   10-ounce package, thawed and drained
Celery   5 stalks, minced
Olive oil   ¼ cup
Mushrooms   ½ pound, thinly sliced
Butter   6 tablespoons
Shrimp   1½ pounds, smaller size, peeled and deveined
Fish fillets*   1 pound, firm-fleshed, cut in ½-inch cubes
Chorizo or spicy dry sausage   ½ pound, sliced
Salt   1 teaspoon

Sauté garlic, onions, pepper, artichokes and celery in oil. In separate pan, sauté mushrooms in 2 tablespoons butter. Sauté shrimp separately in 2 more tablespoons butter and sauté fish cubes separately in remaining butter. Place all prepared ingredients in large bowl, sprinkle with salt, and toss. Reserve to be added to rice before serving.
* Chuck prefers butterfish, but any firm-fleshed fish will do. If you should select butterfish, refer to Black Cod Sukiyaki (see Index) for information on how to bone the fillets.

Step 2:   Prepare the rice.

Long grain rice   3 cups
Olive oil   3 tablespoons
Clam juice   8-ounce bottle with water added to make 4 cups
Salt   1 teaspoon
Saffron   ¼ teaspoon dissolved in warm water
Warm water   ½ cup

Sauté rice in oil in large Dutch oven or immense frying pan until translucent. Add clam juice, salt, and saffron dissolved in warm water. Stir and bring to boil. Simmer 30 minutes, then turn off heat, cover, and let rice sit for 20 minutes to steam. Break up rice in separate grains, gently stir in reserved seasoning-vegetable mixture, and carefully reheat to serving temperature. (You might even reheat seasoning-vegetable mixture before adding to rice.) Taste and correct seasoning.

Step 3: Prepare the garnishes.

Small Malaysian prawns or other crustaceans such as crayfish, clams, king crab, prawns 40
Bamboo skewers small, thin, and broken to size of prawns
Butter ½ cup
Vermouth a jigger for each pan full of prawns (optional)

Leaving shell on prawns, straighten and skewer each prawn from tail to head on the belly side. (This prevents prawns from curling into a ball during sautéing.) Sauté 10 prawns gently in 2 tablespoons butter until just cooked, about 4 minutes or until bright red. After 3 minutes, pour in vermouth and steam for 1 minute for flavor, if desired. Add butter as needed. Repeat until all prawns are cooked.

Step 4: Prepare the arrangement.

Lemon wedges garnish
Parsley garnish

On a very large preheated platter (unless silver), place reheated rice with vegetables and artfully arrange prawns vertically around top of rice. Border platter with lemon wedges and sprinkle parsley over rice (but not prawns). Arrange any other personal selection of garnishes. Serve with pride and take your bows—you've earned them! Serves 20.
Note: For ease in preparing this tour de force, prepare the seasonings and vegetables, skewer the prawns, and select and prepare the garnishes early in the day. Begin rice an hour before dinner and blend all ingredients just before serving. (Chuck says this method preserves the texture of the individual ingredients.) Also, serve drawn butter on the side for the seafood delicacies and be creative in your selection of garnishes, choosing colorful ones such as green and red bell pepper slices, artichoke hearts, sliced sautéed mushrooms, and so forth.

Tuna Niçoise

This is a refreshing summer lunch or light supper and served on a silver tray it is elegant. Make your own vinaigrette sauce or use a bottled one, well chilled. A mound of olives in the center of the platter is attractive, or use the olives to divide foods in the arrangement. Add julienned salami, and you will have an antipasto.

Small new potatoes   6, boiled, salted, and sliced
Frozen string beans   10-ounce package, cooked and drained or
   Canned string beans   16-ounce can, cooked and drained
Lettuce   enough leaves to cover platter
Large tomatoes   2, sliced
Large cucumber   1, sliced
Onion   1 tablespoon minced
Tuna   6½-ounce can, drained and flaked
Parsley   1 tablespoon chopped
Anchovies   4, chopped (optional)
Sauce Vinaigrette (see Index)   ½ cup or more
Pimiento-stuffed green olives   garnish
Pitted black olives   garnish
Melba toast

Cook and chill potatoes and green beans. Arrange lettuce leaves on attractive serving platter. In different sections of platter, place several arrangements of potatoes, several of green beans, and intersperse tomato and cucumber slices between these arrangements. Try for a balance of colors. Sprinkle onion, tuna, and parsley over entire arrangement. If you choose to add anchovies, sprinkle them over top. Pour vinaigrette over it all, except the olive mound if you have one. Serve well chilled with melba toast. Serves 4.

Tuna Quesadillas

Tuna   6½-ounce can, drained
Yogurt or sour cream   6 tablespoons
Cheddar cheese   7 tablespoons grated
Pitted black olives   3 tablespoons chopped
Green onions   ¼ cup sliced
Ground cumin   ¼ teaspoon
Flour tortillas   4, approximately 7-inch diameter
Alfalfa sprouts   ¼ cup (optional)

Drain tuna, flake, and mix with 2 tablespoons yogurt, 3 tablespoons cheese, black olives, 3 tablespoons green onions, and cumin. Spread filling down center of flour tortillas. Top filling with alfalfa sprouts. Roll tortilla and place into 8-inch square buttered glass baking dish. Sprinkle remaining cheese over tortillas and bake for 15 to 20 minutes at 300°, or until heated through. Garnish with remaining yogurt spooned down center, and sprinkle with remaining green onions. Serves 4.

Cheese, Chili, and Shrimp Quiche

Green chilies two 4-ounce cans, seeded and cut into thin strips
Monterey Jack cheese 1 pound, grated
Shrimp ½ pound, preferably tiny bay
Eggs 4, beaten
Parsley 2 teaspoons finely chopped
Salt ¼ teaspoon
Bacon 7 slices, crisp and crushed

Line buttered quiche dish or 9-inch pie pan with chilies. Press on sides and bottom as you would a pie crust. Add cheese and shrimp and distribute evenly. Beat eggs with parsley and salt and pour over shrimp. Sprinkle crushed bacon bits on top. Bake at 325° about 40 minutes or until firm. Serve hot or cold. Serves 4 as a main dish or 6 as an appetizer.
Note: Halved cherry tomatoes make a lovely circle around the edge of the quiche and add a nice note. Also, sprinkle with finely chopped parsley.
Fish Substitutions:
  Pacific-Atlantic: flaked salmon, finnan haddie
  Hawaiian: ahi, aku, mahimahi, onaga, uku

Quiche Saumon

Pie shell   one 9-inch, unbaked
Heavy cream   2 cups, scalded
Onion   ¼ cup chopped
Butter   2 tablespoons
Salt   ¾ teaspoon
White pepper   ½ teaspoon
Nutmeg   ⅛ teaspoon
Chives   2 tablespoons chopped
Eggs   4, beaten
Egg yolk   1, beaten with other eggs
Parmesan cheese   ½ cup grated
Egg white   1, unbeaten
Salmon*   ¼ pound, cooked (preferably poached) and flaked

Bake pie shell until partially done, about 10 minutes. Scald cream by bringing to boiling point, but do not permit it to boil. Set aside. Sauté onion in 1 tablespoon butter, adding salt, pepper, nutmeg, and chives while cooking. Pour eggs with extra yolk, onion mixture, and cheese into scalded cream and blend thoroughly. Lightly brush pie shell with unbeaten egg white. Line shell with flaked salmon and pour in custard mixture. Dot custard with remaining butter. Bake at 375° for 35 to 40 minutes, until custard is lightly browned and set. Serve hot or cold. Serves 4 as a main dish or 6 as an appetizer.
* Thinly sliced smoked salmon is divine. If used, garnish quiche with two thin slices added to top of custard about 20 minutes into cooking. However, this should be served hot so smoked salmon will not become tough.

Gumbo
and
Chowder

Fish and Sausage Gumbo

If you have a touch of the South, you save your bacon grease. You also know that a gumbo is a very special dish from the bayou kitchens. The secret of any successful gumbo is a nicely browned roux, and the secret of this particular gumbo is the stock used. I prefer sea bass or snapper in this stew, but the catch of the day would be fine. Finally, if you're unable to find filé, don't worry, the gumbo will still be authentic—and delicious.

Kielbasa 1 pound, cut in ½-inch widths
Chicken stock* 3 cups
Water 2 cups
Bacon grease ⅓ cup
Flour ⅓ cup plus 2 tablespoons
Large onion 1, chopped
Garlic cloves 2, pressed
Parsley 3 tablespoons chopped
Salt 1 to 2 teaspoons, depending on taste
White pepper ¾ teaspoon
Cayenne ¼ teaspoon
Stewed tomatoes 16-ounce can, chopped with liquid
Fresh okra 1 pound, trimmed and cut or
    Frozen okra two 10-ounce packages, thawed and cut
Shrimp ½ pound, 50 to 60 per pound, shelled and deveined
Fish fillets ½ pound boned, cut in bite-sized pieces
Fresh oysters 1 pint with liquor
Rice
Filé powder 1¼ teaspoons
Green onions 3, thinly sliced, green portion only

Place kielbasa on platter lined with paper towels and microwave for 5 minutes at 70%, or cook in a preheated 375° oven for 20 minutes. Drain on paper towels and set aside. Combine chicken stock and water and set aside. Heat bacon grease over medium-high heat in large Dutch oven. Sprinkle in flour and reduce heat to medium. Stir constantly for 5 minutes. Add onions and garlic and continue stirring for another 5 minutes. Now turn heat to medium-low and stir for 8 minutes. The roux will become a light brown and almost pastelike. (Don't let it burn; keep stirring.) Gradually pour in broth mixture, 1 cup at a time, stirring thoroughly until thickened. Stir in parsley, salt, pepper, and cayenne. Pour in tomatoes and tomato liquid, cover, and simmer 30 minutes. (At this point, you may refrigerate covered pan and kielbasa. Remove from refrigerator 45 minutes before dinner and reheat gumbo over medium heat, stirring frequently.) Add okra to gumbo 35 minutes before dinner, cook over medium-high, and stir occasionally. Add shrimp, fish, oysters plus liquor, and kielbasa to gumbo 15 minutes before dinner. Stir and cover and continue cooking over medium to medium-high heat, stirring once or twice. Scoop about ½ cup of rice into individual soup bowls, and sprinkle ⅛ teaspoon filé powder over each serving. Gently ladle gumbo into bowls and garnish each with a portion of green onions. Serves 10.

* Homemade stock is the best choice for this recipe, although you can use canned chicken broth. I prepare the stock for gumbo a day or so in advance by tossing 1 to 2 pounds of chicken wings into 2 quarts of water along with chopped carrot, some celery leaves, an onion cut in large chunks, 1 whole bay leaf, 5 peppercorns, and ¾ teaspoon salt. After simmering the wings for several hours, I remove them (using the meat for dinner), strain the stock, and chill it overnight. When I'm ready to prepare the gumbo, I spoon and discard the refrigerated fat from the stock and voilà—a sublime chicken stock!

Note: As you can see, much of the preparation can be done far in advance of the evening's meal. Serve with a crusty French bread, Cucumbers with Sour Cream (see Index), and for dessert, a bowl of fruit and cheese.

Fish Substitutions:

Pacific-Atlantic: rockfish, snapper, sea bass, cod, halibut

Hawaiian: rock cod, weke-ula, uku, muu

Uncle Jack's Fish Gumbo

Uncle Jack, like most good fishermen, knows to use the whole fish. After filleting a large bass, he boils the carcass, then lets it cool. Next he strains the stock and removes any meat left on the bones. You can make this gumbo with any fish carcass. Mahimahi is good in Hawaii, but a weke-ula will do just as nicely. Like any gumbo, you must allow the flour to brown.

Bacon grease   6 tablespoons
Flour   ¼ cup
Large onion   1, chopped
Fresh okra   8 to 10, sliced or
    Frozen okra   10-ounce package, thawed
Tomatoes   two 16-ounce cans, with liquid
Celery   2 stalks, chopped
Carrots   3, sliced
Fish stock   2 cups
Fish   meat removed from carcass
Salt and pepper   to taste
Basil   ⅛ teaspoon
Marjoram   ⅛ teaspoon
Tabasco   4 drops
Rice

Heat grease, add flour, and cook until dark brown. After roux has browned, add chopped onion and simmer. Stir okra into roux until coated. Add tomatoes, celery, carrots, fish stock, and fish meat. Stir and add remaining ingredients. Simmer for 2 hours or more. Serve over white rice with hot cornbread. Serves 6 to 8.

Boston Clam Chowder

This chowder is to be made the day before and refrigerated overnight so that the flavors blend. If you want to get fancy, throw in a shot of sherry at the end!

Medium onion   1, diced (about 10 tablespoons)
Medium green bell pepper   1, diced (about 7 tablespoons)
Garlic cloves   2, pressed
Potatoes   2½ cups, cubed (about 4 or 5 medium-large)
Razor clams*   24
Clam liquor   2½ cups, strained broth plus bottled (if necessary)
Bacon   4 slices, bacon grease reserved
Salt   1 teaspoon
Large bay leaf   1
White pepper   ½ teaspoon
Ground thyme   ¼ teaspoon
Butter   1 tablespoon
Milk   2 cups
Heavy cream   ½ cup
Bacon   garnish
Parsley   garnish

Cut all vegetables and set aside (cover cubed potatoes with cold water to prevent discoloration). Steam clams until open. Mince or grind hard part of clams and chop softer parts. Discard neck sheath. Keep hard and soft parts separate. Reserve broth. Fry bacon in Dutch oven over medium heat until crisp. Remove, cool, break into bits, and set aside for later use. In heated bacon grease, add onions, green pepper, and garlic, and sauté over medium-high heat, stirring until onions are translucent. Reduce heat to medium. Add potatoes and minced hard portions of clams. Stir, sprinkle salt over mixture, and stir again. Strain reserved clam broth, adding enough bottled clam juice (if necessary) to make 2½ cups, and add to chowder. Stir in bay leaf, pepper, thyme, and butter. Cover and simmer over low heat for 30 minutes. Meanwhile, scald milk and cream, stirring frequently; do not allow to boil. Set aside until previous simmering time is over. Then remove bay leaf and pour in scalded milk and cream, and add soft clam portions. Refrigerate covered overnight. When ready next day, skim accumulated fat from chowder surface and reheat over medium heat for 30 minutes, stirring frequently (do not allow to boil). Serve in heated bowls, stir in reserved bacon bits, and garnish with more bacon bits and/or minced parsley. Serves 8.
* If you should use steamers, allow 36. Of course, the canned baby boiled clams mixed with minced clams will work also.

New England Fish Chowder

I like this chowder because it may be made ahead of time and it cooks in the oven.
You may combine everything to the point of baking and refrigerate the casserole.

Cod or any white fish   2 pounds, cut in chunks
Potatoes   4, peeled and sliced
Onions   3, peeled and sliced
Butter   ½ cup
Dry white wine   ½ cup
Boiling water   2 cups
Garlic clove   1, squeezed
Bay leaf   1
Salt   2 teaspoons or less, depending on taste
White pepper   ⅛ teaspoon
Whole cloves   3
Dill weed   1 teaspoon
Parsley   1 teaspoon minced
Dried lemon peel   ¼ teaspoon ground or
    Fresh lemon peel   ½ teaspoon minced
Light cream   2 cups, scalded
Chives   garnish
Paprika   garnish

Combine all ingredients but the scalded cream in 3-quart casserole.
Cover and bake 1 hour at 350°. (Allow an extra 10 minutes if the casserole
has been refrigerated.) Stir in scalded cream. Garnish with chopped
chives and paprika. Serves 8.

Vegetable Clam Chowder

Vegetable soup lovers will enjoy Leslie Connolly's version of Manhattan clam chowder. Leslie lives in Pennsylvania, and on cold winter nights she dishes this out to her family along with grilled cheese sandwiches.

Baby clams two 6-ounce cans
Clam liquor 2 cups, reserved from cans plus water to make required amount
Bacon 4 slices
Medium onions 2, chopped
Clam juice 8-ounce bottle
Medium potatoes 2, peeled and cubed
Celery 1 stalk, diced
Medium carrots 2, cubed
Tomatoes 16-ounce can, chopped with liquid
V-8 juice 6-ounce can
Fresh green beans 1 cup trimmed to 1 inch (optional)
Parsley 2 tablespoons chopped
Salt 1 teaspoon
White pepper ¼ to ½ teaspoon
Ground thyme ½ teaspoon
Basil ½ teaspoon

Open clams, drain juice into measuring cup, and add water to make 2 cups. Line bottom of Dutch oven with bacon, add onions, and fry with bacon. Pour in clam juice and strained clam liquor, add potatoes, and bring to boil. Cover and simmer for 10 minutes. Add remaining ingredients (except clams), stir, and simmer for 1 hour. Remove strips of bacon and add clams. Heat through and serve. Serves 6 to 8.

Crepes, Appetizers, and Hors d'Oeuvres

Your Basic Crepe

When making crepes you'll find yourself confronted with this dilemma—the thinner the crepe the better, and *the thinner the crepe the harder to cook. If this is your first time with crepes, opt for the larger amount of batter (it will cover the bottom of the pan more easily), and be sure to keep the heat from getting too high (the batter will cook before it covers the pan). One final tip for success: if you're using a pan smaller than 8 inches, be sure to decrease the batter accordingly.*

Butter   2 tablespoons, melted
Eggs   3, beaten
Milk   1½ cups
Flour   1¼ cups
Salt   ⅛ teaspoon
Vegetable oil   ¼ teaspoon

Beat eggs with milk and combine all ingredients in blender and mix well. Allow batter to stand at room temperature for 2 hours. If batter has been refrigerated from previous day, allow to return to room temperature before cooking. Blend again just before using. Heat an 8-inch, nonstick omelet pan over medium-high heat. Brush pan with oil before cooking first crepe (after that, it should be unnecessary). Remove pan from heat, pour in 2 or 3 tablespoons of batter, and immediately swirl pan so that crepe covers bottom and even runs up sides of pan. Return pan to heat and cook until edges brown—about 50 seconds for 3 tablespoons or 35 seconds for 2 tablespoons. When a spatula slides easily under crepe, it is done. Turn crepe and cook other side for another 30 seconds for 3 tablespoons or 15 seconds for 2 tablespoons. Remove crepe to platter and begin again. Makes about 15.

Note: It is unlikely you will need all 15 crepes for one serving, so plan to freeze those you don't use. To freeze, simply layer waxed paper between crepes and wrap tightly in freezer bags. They will last up to 4 months.

Create Your Own Crepe

For those who enjoy cooking creatively, crepes afford a marvelous opportunity for expressing one's individuality. Seafood and crepes complement each other, so in making your own, you may add the seafood filling of your choice. It's a wonderful way to dress up tuna. All that is basically required are chunks of fish or shellfish, a sauce, and a crepe. For example, combine ½ cup of Mornay Sauce (see Index), sautéed mushrooms and shallots, and tiny shrimp. Stuff the crepe, cover with more Mornay Sauce, and heat in an oven for 10 to 15 minutes (or even under the broiler) to lightly brown the top.

In fact, you don't even need to make the sauce. For example, make the Snapper à la King (see Index), but withhold half of the soup and liquid, or enough to bind the filling together. Place a tablespoon or more of the thick Snapper à la King on the crepe and roll, and spoon the remaining portion of the soup-liquid over the top. Don't drown the crepe, of course; spoon the sauce down the middle. Or use the Spinach-Mushroom Mix or Seafood Mix (see Index) to make divine crepes.

The important point is that you can make any kind of crepe you want with any ingredients you like. The key is to add some sauce to the filling, usually ½ cup, and reserve some sauce to spoon over the crepes. Here are some suggestions for ingredients: mushrooms, onions, celery, cheese, spinach, asparagus tips, pimientos, hard-cooked eggs, parsley, and any shellfish or fish. Have fun!

Buffet Gateau

This is another of Enid's famous party dishes, and true to form, everything is made ahead of time. When the gateau is complete, it looks something like a small layered cake. It is rich, so when you serve it, cut in small wedges. Baked tomatoes and deviled eggs are nice complements to the gateau.

Crepes (see Index)   ten 8-inch
Spinach Filling
Mushroom Filling
Mornay Sauce (see Index)   2 cups
Parsley   garnish

In a buttered shallow baking dish or buttered ovenproof platter on which you plan to serve, place a crepe and spread with ⅕ of Spinach Filling. Top with another crepe and gently spread it with ¼ of Mushroom Filling. Repeat, ending with a nicely browned crepe on top. You may cover and refrigerate at this point, if you wish. When ready to serve, cover with sauce and bake at 350° for 25 to 30 minutes, or until hot in center. (Or microwave for 15 minutes at 40%; rotate dish a half-turn and microwave for another 15 minutes at 40% or until heated through. Garnish with chopped parsley and serve. Serves 8.

Spinach Filling

Frozen spinach two 10-ounce packages, thawed or
   Fresh spinach 1½ cups blanched
Onion 2 tablespoons grated
Butter 2 tablespoons
Salt ¼ teaspoon
Parsley 2 teaspoons minced
Mornay Sauce (see Index) ½ cup
Tiny cocktail shrimp* ½ pound or
   Canned shrimp two 4½-ounce cans, drained and rinsed

Squeeze spinach dry, wringing out all water. Lightly sauté onion in butter. Add spinach, salt, and parsley and stir over moderately high heat for 2 or 3 minutes. Fold in sauce and shrimp. Makes approximately 3½ cups.
* Crab or lobster may be readily substituted for the shrimp.

Mushroom Filling

Mushrooms ⅓ pound, preferably smaller ones, thinly sliced
Green onion 1 tablespoon minced
Butter 1 tablespoon
Oil ½ tablespoon
Cream cheese 8-ounce package
Egg 1, beaten
Salt and pepper to taste
Gruyère cheese ½ cup shredded
Parsley 2 teaspoons minced

Sauté mushrooms and onions in butter and oil. Cut cream cheese in small sections, mash, and add to mixture, along with remaining ingredients. Heat until well blended. Makes 3 to 3½ cups.

Other Appetizers and Hors d'Oeuvres

Located in other sections of this book (see Index) are entrées that also make superb appetizers or hors d'oeuvres. Below are some of them listed in alphabetical order.

Calamari

Cheese, Chili, and Shrimp Quiche

Crab with Mousseline Sauce
    in Ramekins

Gravlax

Hawaiian-Style Ceviche

Lingcod Fish Fry

Linguine with White Clam Sauce

Oven-Steamed Oysters

Quiche Saumon

Shrimp Coquilles with
    Mousseline Sauce

Shrimp Tempura

Tuna Niçoise

Cherry Tomatoes Stuffed with Shrimp

My zany neighbor, Joan Chang, has more parties in a month than most people have in a year. Consequently, she has mastered a host of hors d'oeuvres, and this is one of her favorites. It is also a good filling for pastry puffs.

Shrimp   6-ounce can tiny size, drained and rinsed
Curry powder   1 teaspoon
Mayonnaise   2 tablespoons
Horseradish   1 teaspoon, creamed style
Lemon juice   ¼ teaspoon
Cherry tomatoes   2 baskets, rinsed, slightly split with an X across the top
Watercress   garnish
Ti leaves   garnish

Pat shrimp dry with paper towels. Mix curry, mayonnaise, horseradish, and lemon juice. Add shrimp and toss well. Stuff each tomato and arrange on serving tray lined with watercress, ti leaves, or doily. Cover and chill until ready to serve. Makes 36 to 40.

Curried Shrimp Puffs

Shrimp   two 6-ounce cans, drained, rinsed, and finely chopped
Mayonnaise   ¼ cup
Curry powder   2 teaspoons
Celery   2 tablespoons diced
Chives   2 teaspoons finely chopped
Hors d'Oeuvre Puff Shells

Combine first 5 ingredients and chill. Split puffs at side and fill each with about 1 teaspoon of filling. Chill before serving. To serve refrigerated filled puffs, place puffs in preheated 450° oven for 1 to 2 minutes. (This heats the puff, without heating the filling.) Makes 48.
Variations: The fillings may be varied by using crab, lobster, sardines, tuna, or salmon.
Note: These puffs may be made in advance of a party. A whole, tiny bay shrimp placed upon the filling in each puff adds to the elegance. In Hawaii, I serve these on ti leaves, but doilies, parsley clumps, or a bed of watercress would serve equally well.

Hors d'Oeuvre Puff Shells

Water   1 cup
Butter   ½ cup
All-purpose flour   1 cup sifted
Eggs   4

Lightly grease 2 cookie sheets and set aside. In large saucepan bring water to boiling. Add butter, reduce heat, and stir until butter is melted. Over low heat, dump all flour at once into water. Stir vigorously with wooden spoon until batter forms a ball around spoon and leaves sides of pan. Remove from heat at once. Add eggs, one at a time, and beat batter hard after each addition. Continue until blended well. Drop mixture by rounded teaspoons onto greased cookie sheets, leaving a 2-inch space between them. Bake in preheated 450° oven for 5 minutes. Reduce heat to 375° and continue baking for another 20 to 25 minutes, until puffs are dry looking, slightly golden, and sides feel rigid. Cool. (Unfilled puffs may be stored in an airtight container for several days or frozen. If refrigerating unfilled puffs, slice them first.) Makes 48.

Savory Clam Puffs

Bread rounds   24, toasted on one side
Cream cheese   4 ounces
Butter   ¼ cup, melted
Minced clams   two 6½-ounce cans, drained
Savory   ¼ teaspoon
Worcestershire sauce   1 teaspoon
Salt   ¼ teaspoon
White pepper   ⅛ teaspoon
Onion powder   ¼ teaspoon
Lemon peel   ½ teaspoon grated
Parsley   1 tablespoon minced
Parsley   garnish

Mix all ingredients except bread and garnish. Spread generous portion of mixture on toasted side of bread and arrange on cookie sheet. Broil until puffy, about 4 inches from medium heat. Sprinkle with garnish and serve immediately. Makes 24.
Variations: Crab may be substituted for clams, and Pickapeppa Sauce may be substituted for Worcestershire.

Sunday Afternoon Lobster

In the days when lobster was a bit less expensive, I used to serve this on a late Sunday afternoon. Sunday afternoons always had a melancholy about them, and this dish seemed to enliven our spirits. It was also a welcome treat on those days of never-ending sporting events, such as New Year's Day. Suddenly we heard family and friends discussing lobster instead of passes.

Butter   ½ cup
Parsley-Garlic Mix (see Index)   3 tablespoons
Salt   to taste
Lobster tails*   twelve, 2-ounce each, cut in chunks
Parmesan cheese   ¼ cup grated
French bread

In a large frying pan heat butter over medium to medium-high heat. Add Parsley-Garlic Mix, salt, and lobster tails. Cook over medium heat, stirring constantly, for about 7 to 10 minutes or until the flesh is bright red and white. (Shrimp will require only about 4 minutes.) Sprinkle cheese into mixture and stir. Serve hot with crusty French bread slices for dunking into sauce. Serves 6.

* If you use frozen lobster tails, cut them while they are still partially frozen; it's easier. If you substitute shelled shrimp for the lobster, cut the larger shrimp into two pieces or leave the medium shrimp whole.

Poached Oysters in Spinach Leaves

This is another of Sheldon Zane's superb creations. It originated with Chef Georges Paineous who has Le Bretagne restaurant in Brittany, France. (The Zanes have a way of discovering small inns which offer lodging and are known for their cuisines.) Of course, Sheldon speaks French, so they are able to make their way fairly easily. In case you speak French, he says this dish is called "Pockets d'Huîtres pochés au jus naturel au beurre limon."

Small oysters 3 to 4 per person
Oyster liquor reserved and strained
Large spinach leaves 1 per oyster
Unsalted butter ½ cup
Lemon juice from 1 lemon

Shuck oysters and save liquor. Squeeze ⅓ lemon juice over oysters. Wrap oysters individually in spinach leaf and place in ovenproof pan. Pour strained oyster liquor over wrapped oysters and place pan over stove until liquor boils, about 1 to 2 minutes. Immediately place pan in 450° oven for 2 minutes. Melt butter, add ⅔ lemon juice, and whisk or stir well. Arrange 3 to 4 oysters on individual plates and surround with lemon-butter sauce.

Mousseline (Quenelle) St. Jacques

This is another of the Zanes' first choices as a first course.

Scallops   ½ cup
Egg white   1
Egg   1
Cream   1 cup
Nutmeg   dash
Fish fumet*   ½ cup
Egg yolk   1
Basil leaves   ¾ teaspoon

Combine first 5 ingredients in a blender. Pour ⅔ full into 4 well-greased ramekins. Place ramekins in pan and fill with boiling water halfway up the side of the ramekins. Place pan in 350° oven for 20 minutes. To make the sauce, combine fumet, egg yolk, and basil in a saucepan and heat, whisking continually, until sauce is thickened to the consistency of light maple syrup. When ramekins are done, invert individually on a plate and surround with sauce. Serves 4.

* Fumet is concentrated fish stock. It is made like the Court-Bouillon (see Index), but fish bones and trimmings are required. Decrease water to 1½ cups and increase white wine to 1 cup. Bring to a boil and simmer uncovered for 1 hour until stock is concentrated. Strain and use.

Crispy Wun Tun

Ground pork ½ pound
Shrimp ¼ pound, cleaned and chopped
Large Chinese water chestnuts 2, peeled and chopped
Green onions 2, green top portions only, chopped
Egg yolk 1, white reserved
Cornstarch ¼ teaspoon
Soy sauce 2 teaspoons
Sherry or bourbon 1 teaspoon
Wun tun pi 10-ounce package
Oil for deep frying
Chinese Dipping Sauce

Mix first 8 ingredients in food processor. Spoon ½ teaspoon of mixture into each wun tun wrapper. Paint reserved egg white on 2 edges of square, fold into triangle, and seal edges by pressing. Bring together and overlap 2 opposite corners; paint with a little egg white and press together. Now bring tip of triangle to meet other corners and pinch together; you may even give a little quick twist. Deep fry about 10 at a time at 350° for about 2 to 3 minutes. Drain on paper towels. Serve with Chinese Dipping Sauce. Makes 36.
Note: These may be refrigerated and later reheated on a brown paper bag on a cookie sheet in a 400° oven until heated through, about 10 minutes.

Chinese Dipping Sauce

Soy sauce ½ cup
Hot Chinese mustard to taste

Mix soy sauce with desired amount of hot Chinese mustard. The more mustard, the hotter it is. Stir thoroughly before serving. Makes ½ cup.

Hawaiian Fish Balls

These are great hot party appetizers. You may make them ahead and reheat them on a brown paper bag in a 400° oven for 10 minutes if you wish.

Fish fillets*   1 pound boned and in pieces
Green onion   2 stalks
Watercress   six 3-inch tips
Chinese parsley   1 teaspoon
Salt   ½ teaspoon
White pepper   ¼ teaspoon
Ginger   1 teaspoon
Cornstarch   2 teaspoons
Red chili pepper   ½ teaspoon minced or
    Dried crushed red pepper   ¼ teaspoon
Vegetable oil, 2 tablespoons, preferably sesame
Soy sauce   1 tablespoon
Sherry or bourbon   1 tablespoon
Egg   1
Corn oil or shortening   to fry
Chinese Dipping Sauce (see Index)   ½ cup

Blend all ingredients, except corn oil and sauce, in food processor for 1 minute. Place mixture in bowl and cover. Chill for at least 1 hour. Patting your hands in flour and removing excess, shape a small ball about the size of a rubber jack ball. (Flour hands before shaping each ball.) Preheat a heavy frying pan and heat oil to about 370°. Don't let it smoke. Add enough oil to form a 2-inch layer in pan. Fry balls until golden—only a few minutes, turning as needed. Drain on paper towels and serve hot with sauce. (Serve sauce in a bowl for dipping beside fish balls.) Makes 24.
* You may use any kind of fish fillet, as long as you remove the bones. I prefer butterfish (for boning butterfish, see Black Cod Sukiyaki), but cod or salmon would work equally well.

Christmas Pâté

This delightful, inexpensive party pâté will bring you raves, particularly if you have set it in an attractive mold—for Christmas, a Christmas tree mold is most festive!

Sardines   three 3¾-ounce cans
Butter   ½ cup
Cream cheese   2 ounces
Lemon juice   2 tablespoons plus 2 teaspoons
Onion   1 tablespoon chopped
Parsley   2 tablespoons chopped
Eggs   2, hard-cooked, plus 2 more hard-cooked egg yolks
Hot sauce   ¼ to ½ teaspoon, depending upon taste
Unflavored gelatin   ¼ teaspoon
Cold water   1 tablespoon plus 1 teaspoon
Salt   ¾ teaspoon
White pepper   ¼ teaspoon
Sesame round toast

In food processor, or using electric mixer, combine all ingredients except sesame rounds. Process or beat until mixture is of pâté texture. Pack pâté into buttered 20-ounce mold. Chill well. (If you are running short on time, pop mold into freezer for 1 hour.) Unmold on serving plate by placing plate over top of mold; holding firmly, flip mold over. Gently tap bottom of mold to release pâté. Makes 2½ cups.

Note: There are any number of ways to decorate the pâté. For example, run a straight line of caviar or piped cream cheese from the top of the tree through the center of the base. On one side of the tree sprinkle finely chopped egg whites and on the other, minced egg yolks. Other selections might be chopped pimientos with minced parsley. If you are more artistically inclined, you might pipe the cream cheese so that the tree has an appearance of tinsel from limb to limb. You might even cut a star from the pimiento. Regardless of the decoration, do surround the tree with numerous bunches of parsley, even if it means using a different basket or tray for the sesame rounds.

Spinach-Clam Spread

Recently I was attending a potluck party and as Charmaine Weinberg approached,
I heard murmurings of "Oh, here comes Charmaine, and I bet she has that
delicious spread." Indeed she did!

Frozen chopped spinach*   two 10-ounce packages, thawed and
    squeezed dry
Cream cheese   8-ounce package, softened
Onion   2 tablespoons grated
Dried onion flakes   1 tablespoon
Lemon juice   1 teaspoon
Clams   6½-ounce can, minced and drained
Salt and pepper   to taste
Mayonnaise   enough to make mixture spreadable
Tabasco   dash (optional)

Blend ingredients and mix well. Cover and refrigerate. (The spread will
keep covered in a refrigerator for 2 weeks.) Makes approximately
3½ cups.
* The secret of this spread is to defrost the spinach thoroughly and
squeeze every drop of water from it. Defrosting the spinach requires
time, so place it in the refrigerator the night before and the next day, place
it in the sink. The spinach is used uncooked.
Variations: This spread is good lightly broiled on crackers or warmed
and served on a baked potato. It may also be served in stuffed manicotti or
a crepe. You may substitute baby shrimp for the clams if you prefer.

Crab Mousse

Olive Brown makes this marvelous mousse on a Thursday for her party on
Saturday. On Sunday morning she adds any left over to eggs and makes a divine
omelet.

Unflavored gelatin   1 tablespoon
Water   ½ cup
Cream cheese   8-ounce package
Condensed cream of chicken soup   10¾-ounce can
Fresh or canned crab meat   6½ ounces
Green onions   ½ cup chopped, including tops
Celery   ½ cup diced
Tabasco   2 dashes

Dissolve gelatin in water. Melt cream cheese with chicken soup. Mix all ingredients together and pour into greased 1-quart mold. Chill until firm and unmold on serving tray. Makes 4 cups.

Shrimp Mousse

This is particularly attractive when prepared in a fish mold.

Condensed cream of tomato soup   10¾-ounce can
Salt   ¼ teaspoon
Unflavored gelatin   1 tablespoon
Cold water   ¼ cup
Cream cheese   8-ounce package, softened
Shrimp   two 6-ounce cans, rinsed, drained, and cut in small pieces
Onion   ¾ cup minced
Scallions   ¼ cup thinly sliced, including green tops
Celery   1 cup minced
Mayonnaise   1 cup
Horseradish   1 teaspoon
Parsley   garnish
Cucumber slices   garnish

Place soup and salt in pan and heat to boiling. Soften gelatin in cold water for 5 minutes. Add softened gelatin and cream cheese to soup, stir, and cool. Add remaining ingredients, except parsley and cucumber, and stir thoroughly. Pack in buttered 2-quart mold and chill until firm, at least 4 hours. Unmold on chilled flat serving tray. Garnish with parsley and cucumber slices. Makes about 7¾ cups.

Caviar

Caviar, or fish roe, lends a feeling of elegance to any affair. While there are numerous variations in serving, I prefer it the classic way—straight—but sometimes that's not feasible. In those instances a dab on canapés or a spread goes a long way.

There are also different kinds of caviar, but essentially the gray/black ones are interchangeable. The most highly prized is the sturgeon roe, but few can afford that. Check your gourmet section for lumpfish or whitefish caviar.

Finally, caviar is highly perishable. Keep it refrigerated, but not frozen. When serving, place the small bowl of caviar in a larger bowl filled with cracked ice. Also, if the caviar has excessive black ink, drain carefully, leaving the liquid in the jar.

Caviar Classic

Caviar   7-ounce jar
Lemon wedges   from 2 lemons
Eggs   3, hard-cooked, finely chopped
Liverwurst   8 ounces
Cream cheese*   8-ounce package, softened
Crackers   (rye, sesame rounds, Norwegian flatbread, wheat thins, etc.)

Carefully empty caviar into bowl. Chill well. Place lemon wedges in small bowl and eggs in separate bowl with a demitasse spoon. On each side of caviar offer a mound of liverwurst and of cream cheese, each with their respective spreaders. Allow guests to serve themselves by creating their own favorites. Makes about 3 cups.
* Herb cheese can be substituted for cream cheese.

Caviar over Cream Cheese

Caviar   4-ounce jar
Cream cheese   8-ounce package, softened
Crackers or toast

Gently pour caviar over softened cream cheese, leaving accumulated black ink in bottom of jar. Serve with a spreader and assorted crackers or melba toast. Makes 1½ cups.

Caviar and Sour Cream Spread

Sour cream ¼ cup
Caviar 7-ounce jar
Lemon juice from ½ lemon, freshly squeezed
Onion 1½ tablespoons grated

Carefully fold sour cream into caviar and mix without breaking the eggs. Add lemon juice and onion and stir well. Chill and serve in a bowl on cracked ice. Makes about 1½ cups.

Caviar and Egg Mousse

My sister, Shirley, sent this to me; it's one of her favorites.

Unflavored gelatin 1 tablespoon
Sherry 2 tablespoons
Lemon juice 2 tablespoons
Eggs 6, hard-cooked, finely minced
Mayonnaise 1 cup
Anchovy paste 1 teaspoon
Parsley 1 tablespoon minced
Worcestershire sauce 1 teaspoon
Onion 1 teaspoon grated
Caviar 2½-ounce jar
Pimiento-stuffed green olives garnish

Soften gelatin in sherry and lemon juice in a small bowl for 5 minutes. Place bowl over water in a small pan or heat in a microwave until gelatin is liquefied. Put eggs through a ricer, food processor, or blender. Mix together next 6 ingredients. Add liquefied gelatin and stir. In 3 strokes, fold in caviar, being careful not to break eggs. Place mixture in a greased 20-ounce mold and chill until firm. Unmold on chilled flat serving tray. Garnish with olives. Makes approximately 2½ cups.

Fish Lady Fingers

This is another favorite concoction of my Uncle Jack of sauger recipe fame.

Shrimp   12 in shell
Court-Bouillon (see Index)   1 quart
Firm-fleshed fish fillets   1 pound, cut in fingers
Watercress   garnish
Lemon slices   garnish
Paprika garnish
Parsley   garnish
Cocktail sauce

Cook shrimp in bouillon, remove, rinse, and chill. Skim or strain bouillon, if necessary, and allow it to cool. Cut fillets in fingers and place in bouillon. Bring it to a boil, remove from heat immediately, and take out fingers. Arrange fingers on a bed of watercress, surrounded by shrimp and lemon slices. Lightly sprinkle with paprika and minced parsley. Serve with cocktail sauce. Makes 15 to 20.
Fish Substitutions:
      Pacific-Atlantic: halibut, bass
      Hawaiian: mahimahi, opakapaka

Anchovy Olives

Pitted large green olives   5- to 10-ounce bottle
Anchovy paste   to fill

Stuff olives with anchovy paste and return to bottle. Cover with their original juice, replace lid and refrigerate overnight.

Swordfish Palau Pupu

Palau is a small island in Micronesia, and "pupu" is the Hawaiian word for hors d'oeuvre. This is really a Micronesian version of ceviche and hails from Jeanne Reinhart who lived in Samoa.

Swordfish   3 pounds, cut in chunks
Fresh lime juice   3 cups
Coconut milk   2 cups
Medium onion   1, diced
Tomatoes   3, finely chopped

Marinate fish in lime juice for 6 hours. Drain and rinse quickly in cold water. Pat dry and add coconut milk, onions, and tomatoes. Toss gently and chill for at least 2 hours before serving. Serves 8.

Note: This may be served in lettuce cups or in chilled champagne or sherbet glasses and garnished with a sprig of mint.

Fish Substitutions:
 Pacific-Atlantic: halibut, sea bass, bluefish
 Hawaiian: mahimahi, opakapaka, onaga

Lomi Lomi Salmon

"Lomi lomi" means massage in the Hawaiian language, and in this appetizer the salted salmon is "massaged" into tiny pieces. This dish is a standard part of any Hawaiian luau, and many like to mix a little of the lomi lomi with the poi. Here the dish would serve as a first course.

Salted salmon*   ½ pound boned, skinned, "massaged" or diced
Medium tomatoes   3, peeled and diced
Parsley   1 tablespoon minced
Medium onion   1, diced
Green onion   2 stalks, thinly sliced
Crushed ice   3 tablespoons

Dice salmon, tomatoes, and onions. Mince parsley and slice green onions. Keep each wrapped separately in refrigerator until ready to serve. Then combine everything but green onions and ice. Mix thoroughly. Add ice at last minute, stir, pour into small, individual serving bowls, and sprinkle with sliced green onions. Serve immediately. Serves 4.

* To make salted salmon, dissolve 1 tablespoon of rock salt in every cup of water. Soak salmon for 20 to 30 minutes.

Hawaiian-Style Ceviche

Caroline Oda introduced this incredibly delicious, unusual salad as the first course for a dinner, and she graciously shared her recipe. In Hawaii, of course, we have access to specialty foods not available elsewhere, such as Ogo Kim Chee. Caroline used the Ogo Kim Chee for this salad, but dried seaweed works equally well. If you can't find dried seaweed at all, make the salad anyway—it's divine.

Swordfish 1 pound, sliced in squares 1 by ¼-inch thick
Medium onion* 1, thinly sliced
Cucumbers 2, peeled, seeded, and thinly sliced
Fresh lime juice ½ cup
Sugar 1 tablespoon
Olive oil 1 tablespoon
Salt ½ teaspoon
Garlic clove 1, crushed
Small red chili pepper 1, diced and seeded, about 2 teaspoons
Dried seaweed 0.35-ounce package, soaked, drained, and sliced or
    Ogo Kim Chee ½ ounce, drained
Green pepper 1, sliced in rings
Lime slices garnish
Chinese parsley or parsley 1 teaspoon chopped

Combine first 9 ingredients in glass bowl. Toss well, cover, and refrigerate overnight. Stir once or twice. The next day, prepare seaweed by soaking for 15 minutes or longer in hot water until seaweed is tender. Drain and cut long strips into smaller pieces about ½-inch wide, and add to salad. Cut green pepper into attractive rings, reserving 3 for garnish, and add to salad. Toss well and chill again. Stir occasionally throughout the day. Before serving, arrange lime slices facing outward on the sides of a clear glass bowl. Pour in salad mixture and top with parsley and reserved green pepper slices. Serves 4 to 6.
* Use a sweet onion such as a Maui or Texas; the Bermuda also works.
Note: Caroline gave a tip worth passing on: if you are watching your budget, add celery and other vegetables and decrease the amount of fish.
Fish Substitutions:
    Pacific-Atlantic: scallops, salmon, shark
    Hawaiian: shark (mako)

Latin American Ceviche

My Swedish friend, Kris, serves this with toast as an appetizer.

Firm white fish fillets* 1 pound, cubed or sliced
Fresh lime juice 2 cups
Large onion 1, minced
Pitted green olives 20
Tomatoes 3, peeled and minced
V-8 juice or tomato juice 1 cup
Water ½ cup
Ketchup ½ cup
Olive oil ½ cup
Salt 2 teaspoons
Oregano 1 teaspoon
Tabasco ½ teaspoon
Cilantro ½ teaspoon diced (optional)
Avocado slices garnish
Lemon juice garnish

Cut fish into scallop-sized cubes or thin slices. Marinate 3 hours in lime juice, turning occasionally. Drain and rinse quickly in cold water. Add next 11 ingredients, toss gently, and chill well. Garnish with avocado slices dipped in lemon juice. Serves 8.
* You may use any firm white fish fillets, but Kris prefers petrale sole. Swordfish is also excellent in ceviche as are the more expensive scallops.

Sashimi

Sashimi is a delicacy treasured by those who have learned to savor the refreshing taste of raw fish. And that's what sashimi is—fresh, thinly sliced, uncooked fish. A platter of sashimi will disappear faster than any other hors d'oeuvre, except shrimp tempura. Usually the sliced fish is placed like a row of fallen dominoes on a bed of shredded daikon. The daikon also is dipped in the sashimi sauce and eaten. "St. Charles" even arranges his sashimi in the shape of a fish, with each slice looking like a scale.

Daikon   1 large white radish or turnip, shredded
Fish*   ½ pound, steaked or blocked
Soy sauce   ½ cup
Wasabi paste or hot Chinese mustard   ½ to 1 teaspoon, to taste

Shred daikon and arrange on a platter. (Ti leaves or watercress form an attractive backdrop.) Cut away and discard any dark portions of fish. With a very sharp knife, slice *against* grain of fish. If slices are more than 2 inches in length, halve them, so that sashimi appears to be uniform rectangles. Each little slice should be about ⅛-inch thick, about 2 inches in length, and ¾ inch in height. Arrange sashimi, slightly overlapping, on daikon. According to directions on the can of wasabi, add water to powder and allow paste to stand for required amount of time. Pour soy sauce in a shallow bowl and place wasabi paste on the side, or serve small, individual soy sauce dishes with a daub of wasabi placed on edge of dish. Serves 2 to 4. (2 in the Islands, 4 on the mainland).
* The favorite fish for sashimi is the red-fleshed tuna, known in the Islands as *ahi* and *aku*. Onaga, swordfish, and sea bass are other favorites. Halibut is also good, but we don't have that in the Islands. In Hawaii the markets offer the fish cut in blocks designed for sashimi, but any boneless steak will do as well.

Sauces

To Make a Sauce

Below are four ways you can thicken any liquid to make a sauce. First of all, remember to measure your liquid in advance so that you know the amount with which you will be working.

Method 1:   Making a Roux
I use this method more than any other. In a saucepan melt 1 tablespoon of butter and stir in 1 tablespoon of flour until bubbles form, stirring constantly. Gradually add 1 cup of cool liquid and stir until sauce thickens. However, if the liquid is hot, then allow the roux to cool before adding it. This formula of hot plus cool prevents the flour from lumping. Nevertheless, if the flour should lump, strain it; all the lumps are gone and no one will notice the difference.

Method 2:   Using a Beurre Manié
Beurre manié is an efficient way to thicken a sauce and one of my favorites. The advantage of a beurre manié is that you can make as much as you like, roll it in balls measuring 1 tablespoon, and store them in a plastic bag in the refrigerator. You can even freeze them. For each cup of hot liquid to be thickened, you should blend together 1 tablespoon of softened butter plus 1 tablespoon of flour. Remember, beurre manié is basically an *uncooked* roux so it should always be used in conjunction with a hot liquid. Once added to the liquid, the beurre manié should be stirred with a wire whisk until it is completely absorbed into liquid (about 2 minutes) and sauce is thick enough to coat a spoon.

Method 3:   Using Cornstarch
Allow 1 tablespoon of cornstarch for every 2 cups of liquid. Dissolve the cornstarch in a little cold water, then stir it into the heated liquid. Keep stirring until the sauce thickens. However, if cornstarch cooks for too long, it will break down. It gives a translucent quality to its sauces. If you are making only a cup of sauce, allow 1 to 1½ teaspoons of cornstarch.

Method 4:   Using Arrowroot
Arrowroot is my sister's favorite. It provides a delicate texture and preserves the subtle taste of a sauce. However, it cannot be reheated and, like cornstarch, it will break down if overcooked. It is also a little more expensive. Allow 1 tablespoon of arrowroot for every cup of liquid. Like cornstarch, dissolve it in a little cold water before adding to the heated liquid.

A final hint which can be used with a sauce thickened by any of these four methods: you can prevent a film from forming on the top of a sauce by dotting it with flecks of butter. Just stir in the flecks when ready to serve.

Beurre Blanc Sauce

This sauce is representative of the nouvelle cuisine *in that it is not made with flour or other thickeners. But while it has a lighter taste, the calories are still there, folks. This sauce works well served in the manner of* nouvelle cuisine—*that is, served on an individual plate first with the entrée gently placed upon it. Beurre Blanc Sauce is also versatile. It can be a dip for steamed crab claws or legs, and it is very good with poached or steamed fish fillets.*

Shallots   2, finely chopped
Butter   1 tablespoon
White wine   ¼ to ⅓ cup
Salt and white pepper   to taste
Butter   1 cup

Sauté shallots in 1 tablespoon butter. Add wine and a pinch of salt and white pepper. Reduce liquid by ⅔. Keep sauce simmering, and add 1 cup butter without boiling. Using a wire whisk, whip mixture vigorously, without stopping, until sauce becomes very foamy and white. Makes 1⅔ cups.

Court-Bouillon

Court-Bouillon is the best poaching liquid for fish. It imparts a delicate flavor to the fish without overwhelming it, and it's easy and inexpensive to make.

Water   1 quart
White wine   ½ cup
Salt   ¾ teaspoon
Peppercorns   6, crushed or cracked
Lemon juice   1 tablespoon
Celery   1 stalk with leaves, cut in chunks
Large carrot   1, cut in chunks
Large bay leaf   1
Parsley   1 large sprig
Leeks   two 3-inch sections of green only, rinsed or
   Small onion   ½
Fish trimmings*   (optional)

Combine all ingredients in a large pot and bring to a boil. Reduce heat and simmer uncovered for 20 minutes (or microwave for 20 minutes at 50%). Strain and reserve liquid for poaching or for making sauces. Makes 1 quart.
* While it is preferable to use fish trimmings such as the head, fins, tail, and large bones, it is not necessary. (Often we buy our fish already filleted or in steaks, so there aren't any trimmings.) If you do add fish trimmings, add them at the boil state and add another 30 minutes to simmer time (or microwave for an additional 12 minutes at 100%).
Note: You do not have to strain the bouillon before you poach a fish in it. Just wrap the fish in cheesecloth and it will protect the fish and act as its own strainer. Cooking time for fish that is poached in the bouillon is approximately 10 minutes for each 1 inch of thickness.

Velouté Sauce*

A Velouté Sauce is nothing more than a thickened Court-Bouillon and is undoubt-edly the best sauce for fish. There are several formal methods, some requiring mushroom peelings, some requiring simmering in a double boiler for an hour or so. However, I rarely ever have that kind of time, and you probably don't either. Thus, I've found this method to work very well.

Butter   1 tablespoon
Flour   1 tablespoon
Court-Bouillon (see Index)   1 cup

In a saucepan melt butter and add flour, stirring over medium-high heat until roux forms and flour bubbles but does not brown. Gradually add bouillon, stirring constantly. (If it helps you control the sauce, remove saucepan from heat when you first add bouillon.) Stir constantly over medium heat until thickened. Makes 1 cup.
* If you prefer, you may thicken the sauce with a Beurre Manié, a corn-starch, or an arrowroot base rather than the roux (see Index).
Variation: If you add crushed capers, you will have a Caper Sauce, and if you add sautéed shallots, you will have a Bercy Sauce.

Velouté on a Grand Scale

If you have just used a Court-Bouillon for poaching, make 3½ cups of Velouté Sauce and freeze it in 1-cup or ½-cup portions, depending upon the number in your family. Of course, I have five in my family, but only two of us eat sauce, so ½-cup portions serve well. This allows ¼ cup per person. To make such a large amount, I use a Beurre Manié for the microwave or a roux for the Dutch oven. Here is the microwave version.

Beurre Manié (see Index)   8 tablespoons
Court-Bouillon (see Index)   3½ to 4 cups, heated

Add 3 tablespoons of Beurre Manié to heated bouillon; stir and micro-wave on high for 2 minutes. Stir and add another 3 tablespoons of Beurre Manié and microwave on high for another 2 minutes. Add remaining 2 tablespoons of Beurre Manié, microwave on high for 4 minutes, bring-ing the sauce to bubbling. Stir well and dot top with flecks of butter. Allow sauce to cool. Freeze in 1-cup or ½-cup portions. Makes 3½ cups.

Hot Garlic Butter

Butter   2 tablespoons
Garlic clove   1, pressed
Dry white wine   ¾ teaspoon (optional)

Melt butter in saucepan on medium heat, add garlic and wine, and mix until heated. (If microwaving, melt butter at 70%, pour off clarified butter, add garlic and wine and quickly reheat at 70%.) Makes 2 tablespoons (1 individual serving).

Tempura Sauce

Tempura Sauce is based on a Japanese broth known as "dashi." The central ingredient for dashi is dried bonito flakes. There are several ways of preparing this sauce, but the simplest is to use the packages of dashi soup stock.

Dashi-no-moto soup stock*   1 small packet (10 grams) or teabag
Water   2 cups
Soy sauce   1 tablespoon
Mirin   1 tablespoon (optional)
Sugar   ½ teaspoon
Salt   ½ teaspoon
Green onion   1 tablespoon of white and green portions thinly sliced
Daikon   ½ cup shredded

Add soup stock to water and boil until dissolved (or microwave at 100% for 5 minutes). Add soy sauce, mirin, sugar, and salt and bring to another boil. Cool. Pour into serving bowl until you see sediment; stop. Set sauce aside at room temperature until ready to serve. Just before serving, sprinkle green onion and daikon over sauce. Makes 1¼ cups.
* The soup stock may come in tea bag form, or in small aluminum packets containing a crushed bouillon mixture. Either is easy to use, but I prefer the packets. If you use the bag, do not squeeze it over the soup, for it will cause cloudiness of the broth.

Cajun Sauce

This is one of my husband's favorite sauces, and each time I serve it—whether with fish or salad—it draws raves. It's particularly good with celeriac, leeks, and Tuna Niçoise.

Tarragon vinegar   2 tablespoons
Paprika   1 teaspoon
Cayenne   ¼ teaspoon
Dijon mustard*   ¾ teaspoon
Salt   ½ teaspoon
Parsley   1 teaspoon minced
Light vegetable oil   6 tablespoons

Combine all ingredients except oil and beat vigorously with a wire whisk. Still beating with whisk, gradually add oil until sauce is well blended. Makes ½ cup.
* Try to use a variety with seeds, such as Maitre Jacques Dijon Grained Mustard with Burgundy Wine (found in the gourmet section of most grocery stores).
Note: If made before using, set aside at room temperature; if refrigerated, rewhip before pouring over salad or fish.

Pesto Sauce

My three-year-old laps up this sauce like a kitten slurping cream. However, she also eats hot peppers and stuffed green olives. Nevertheless, this really is an unusually good sauce, even though it varies from the authentic pesto.

Parsley   3 tablespoons chopped or minced
Watercress   3 tablespoons chopped or minced
Fresh basil   3 tablespoons chopped or minced or
    Dried basil   2 tablespoons
Capers   1 tablespoon
Garlic cloves   2, minced
Salt and white pepper   ¼ teaspoon
Parmesan cheese   2 tablespoons grated
Oil   5 tablespoons, preferably olive
Lemon juice   1 tablespoon

Blend all ingredients except oil and lemon juice until a smooth paste is formed. Add 1 tablespoon of oil at a time, beating constantly with wire whisk, until all 5 tablespoons are absorbed. Continuing to beat mixture, dribble in lemon juice and pour the last tablespoon of oil on the top. Rewhip before serving. Cover tightly and refrigerate. Makes ½ cup.
Note: Put this in a tightly covered glass jar and it will last several weeks in your refrigerator. Be certain to beat again before using. I prefer a food processor for blending the ingredients, but a blender or mortar and pestle or just plain mincing by hand will do the job.

Mousseline Sauce

This is a superb sauce in the tradition of nouvelle cuisine—*I prefer it over hollandaise! Sheldon and Gwen Zane introduced it to me. A wire whisk is essential. Have all ingredients ready before you begin because the sauce cooks very quickly.*

Water   1 tablespoon
White wine vinegar   2 tablespoons
Dry white wine   1 tablespoon
Egg yolks   2
Lemon juice   2 teaspoons
Unsalted butter*   ½ cup
Whipping cream   ¼ cup

In a small saucepan heat water, vinegar, and wine over high heat and reduce for 1 minute. Lower heat to medium and add yolks, juice, and butter. Whisk thoroughly . Add cream, continue whipping, and remove from stove. Serve with any fish or shellfish. Makes 1 cup.
* If butter is unsoftened, cut in five pieces.

White Sauce

I will admit that I have become a fan of the packaged dry mix for white sauce. It's just so easy, and I'm so spoiled. I merely add the additional ingredients to it and voilà! *However, if you wish to make your own, the following will make a medium sauce.*

Butter   2 tablespoons
Flour   2 tablespoons
Milk   1 cup, scalded and cooled
Salt   to taste
Lemon juice   1 teaspoon
Cayenne   ⅛ teaspoon
Parsley   1 tablespoon minced or
    Watercress   1 tablespoon of minced tips or
    Chives   1 tablespoon thinly sliced

Melt butter and add flour, stirring constantly, until flour bubbles. Remove pan from heat and gradually add cooled milk, stirring constantly. Simmer and stir, preferably with a wire whisk, until thickened. Combine remaining ingredients and stir into sauce. Makes 1 cup.

Variations: A can of tiny, drained shrimp will add a touch of elegance for any white sauce. Or add 1 tablespoon of prepared mustard, cook for 5 minutes over low heat, and you have a mustard sauce which is also good with fish.

Simple Hollandaise Sauce

The most simple Hollandaise, of course, is the packaged dry mix, which I rely upon in an emergency. But for those who wish to make their own sauce without fear of curdling, here is a reasonable method.

Arrowroot   2 tablespoons
Lemon juice   1 tablespoon
White wine   2 tablespoons
Butter   ½ cup
Lemon juice   3 tablespoons
Salt   ¼ teaspoon
White pepper   ⅛ teaspoon
Sugar   ¼ teaspoon
Whipping cream   1 cup
Egg yolks   4

Beat arrowroot into lemon juice (1 tablespoon) and white wine until dissolved; set aside. Using saucepan with thick bottom, melt butter over medium heat. (Do not allow butter to brown.) Add 3 tablespoons lemon juice, salt, pepper, and sugar and remove pan from heat. Pour 1 tablespoon whipping cream into egg yolks and lightly whip. Pour remaining whipping cream into sauce. Using wire whisk, whip egg yolk mixture and arrowroot mixture into pan. (Stir arrowroot mixture before addition.) Return pan to medium to medium-high heat and continue to whip vigorously until sauce begins to boil; don't allow it to boil. Remove from heat immediately and serve. Makes 1½ cups.

Mornay Sauce

Butter   3 tablespoons
Flour   ¼ cup
Salt   ¼ teaspoon
White pepper   ½ teaspoon
Chicken broth   1½ cups
Cream   ⅓ cup, scalded and cooled
Gruyère cheese   3 tablespoons shredded
Parmesan cheese   3 tablespoons grated
Parsley   2 teaspoons minced

Melt butter over medium heat and add flour, stirring constantly. Add salt and pepper. Slowly stir in chicken broth and cream. Add cheeses and parsley. Stir well and simmer briefly, until thickened. Makes 2½ cups.

Newburg Sauce

Butter   2 tablespoons
Shallots   2 tablespoons finely chopped
Flour   1 tablespoon
Cream   1¼ cups, scalded and cooled
Chervil   ¾ teaspoon
Cayenne   ⅛ teaspoon
Egg yolks   3, well beaten
Cognac   2 teaspoons (optional)

Melt butter over medium heat and sauté shallots. Sprinkle flour over shallots and stir until butter and flour are well mixed. (Do not let mixture brown.) Gradually add cooled cream, stirring constantly. Add chervil and cayenne, still stirring. When sauce thickens, remove pan from heat. Meanwhile heat water in bottom portion of double boiler, but do not put top portion over water yet. Drop egg yolks into cool top pan. Pour a little sauce into yolks, stirring gently and constantly. Continue to add all sauce. Now place top pan over hot water and cook, stirring gently, for about 3 minutes. Add cognac if desired. Lower heat and keep sauce warm. Makes 1½ cups.

Butter-Wine Sauce

This is the sauce used in the Oven-Steamed Kumu, but it works as well with salmon or other fish.

Butter 3 tablespoons
Lemon juice 3 tablespoons
Dry white wine 3 tablespoons
Garlic cloves* 2, pressed or
    Capers 1 teaspoon chopped
Caper juice dash
Parsley ¾ teaspoon minced

Melt butter and add remaining ingredients. Stir well and simmer until heated through. Makes ¾ cup.
* If the fish you serve has a particularly delicate flavor, such as trout or opakapaka, omit the garlic and substitute capers.

Curry Mayonnaise

This is my husband's favorite; he will eat it with a spoon.

Mayonnaise 1 cup
Curry powder 1 tablespoon

Stir curry into mayonnaise until well blended. Chill. Makes 1 cup.
Note: The kind of mayonnaise you use will "make or break" this recipe, so please use a good, authentic one.

Chilled Cucumber Sauce

Cucumbers ½ cup unpeeled and diced
Salt ½ teaspoon
Lemon juice 1 teaspoon
Onion 1 teaspoon grated
Sugar ¼ teaspoon
Olive oil ¾ cup
Ice cubes 2 or 3
Dry mustard ¼ teaspoon
Black pepper ⅛ teaspoon freshly ground

Cut cucumbers in half lengthwise and scoop out seeds; then dice cucumbers and place in shallow bowl. Sprinkle with salt, cover with waxed paper, and weight cucumbers. Refrigerate for at least 1 hour. Combine lemon juice, onion, and sugar and beat in olive oil gradually with wire whisk. Add 2 or 3 ice cubes and dry mustard and beat with fork. Discard ice. Thoroughly drain cucumbers and stir into sauce. Serve well chilled. Makes 1½ cups.

Chilled Watercress Sauce

Watercress leaves ¼ cup minced
Parsley 1 tablespoon
Mayonnaise 1 cup
Chili sauce 2 tablespoons
Salt to taste

In a food processor or blender, mince watercress. Add remaining ingredients, blend, and chill well. Makes 1½ cups.

Green Mayonnaise

This sauce is particularly ideal for salmon.

Parsley 2 tablespoons
Tarragon leaves 2 tablespoons
Chives 1 tablespoon
Chervil 1 teaspoon
Fresh dill ¾ teaspoon
Mayonnaise 2 cups
Salt and white pepper to taste

Finely chop all herbs or mix in food processor. Blend with mayonnaise and salt and pepper to taste. Chill well for several hours before serving. Makes 2 cups.

Sauce Vinaigrette

This is my favorite vinaigrette sauce. I make it in advance and store it in the refrigerator. However, remove the garlic clove halves after twenty-four hours, or the sauce might be too strong. Also, if you substitute fresh herbs for the dried variety, you won't be able to store the vinaigrette for long—again, the taste will become too strong.

Salt ½ teaspoon
Coarsely ground pepper ½ teaspoon
Dry mustard ½ teaspoon
Tarragon 1 teaspoon
Basil 1 teaspoon
Olive oil 12 tablespoons
Lemon juice 4 tablespoons
Large garlic clove 1, cut in half
Pimientos 1 teaspoon finely chopped

In small bowl combine salt, pepper, mustard, tarragon, basil, 2 tablespoons oil, and 2 tablespoons lemon juice. Beat with wire whisk or fork until smooth. Gradually add another 4 tablespoons oil and beat well again. Add remaining 2 tablespoons of lemon juice and 6 tablespoons oil, pouring oil slowly in a steady stream and whisking constantly. Add garlic halves and pimientos. Pour mixture into jar; cover well and chill thoroughly. Shake well before using. Makes 1 cup.
Variations: For added interest, you may add a variety of other seasonings or specialties such as Roquefort cheese bits, hard-cooked egg bits, or sour cream.

Tartar Sauce

Tarragon   1 teaspoon finely chopped
Shallots   2 teaspoons minced or
    Chives   1 tablespoon finely chopped
Capers   2 tablespoons finely chopped
Sweet pickle   1 tablespoon chopped, preferably gherkins
Dijon mustard   1 teaspoon
Salt and pepper   to taste
Mayonnaise   1 cup
Tarragon vinegar   2 teaspoons or more to thin sauce

Mix together tarragon, shallots, capers, pickle, and mustard. Add salt and coarsely ground pepper to taste. Blend mixture into mayonnaise and thin with vinegar as desired. Makes 1¼ cups.

Blender Aioli Sauce

Olive oil is a must for this sauce! If you wish, you may add the cayenne or a little minced red chili pepper.

Garlic cloves   10 to 12, chopped
Salt   ½ teaspoon
White pepper   ¼ teaspoon
Cayenne   dash (optional)
Egg yolks   3
Lemon juice   3 tablespoons
Olive oil   1½ cups

Puree chopped garlic in blender. Add salt, pepper, cayenne, egg yolks, lemon juice, and ½ cup olive oil. Blend at high speed for 3 seconds or until mixture just thickens. Slowly add remaining oil in thin, steady stream and blend well. If mixture seems too thick, thin with ½ teaspoon water or more. If sauce separates before serving, rebind by beating vigorously with wire whisk, adding small egg yolk if necessary. Serve well chilled. Makes 2 cups.

Entertaining
with Flair

Successful entertaining requires flair. Not only will your guests be wooed by carefully prepared food in interesting menus, but also by the more subtle accompaniments like decor, lighting, music, and so forth. This section of the book aims to help you develop some of this entertaining flair.

In the following pages, you'll find a variety of menus for both formal and casual entertaining—and for different sizes of groups. All seafood entrées and appetizers appear earlier in the book and can be found in the index (asterisks indicate recipes included in the following pages).

Often, you'll find that I recommend a menu item like lemon meringue pie, referring you to your favorite recipe. I think it's always a good idea for a cook, even an experienced one, to rely on at least a recipe or two from an existing repertoire. You'll find, too, that I'm a great believer in simplicity—and that includes considerations like ease of preparation. As often as possible, I've tried to prepare menus that will allow you to do most of your bustling and assembling *before* your guests arrive. This may be the single greatest boon to achieving a pleasurable evening for both guests and hosts.

The Setting

Lights, music, action! Like a good director, you should give some consideration to the backdrop that will set the mood for your party. Naturally, the heart of the evening will be the menu itself, but seating, lighting, decor, and music can make the whole event a show-stopper!

Menu: Budget, time, and seating possibilities will automatically limit your menu choices. For example, you most likely won't serve Fillets of Sole Meunière for twelve because it takes too long to prepare for twelve at the last minute. You wouldn't see much of your guests. Or you won't plan a dinner for twelve if you live in a studio apartment; you might have a picnic, but not a dinner. Like a new suit of clothes, you'll need to look for a comfortable "fit"—i.e., a menu that will wear well in terms of time, effort, and expense.

Seating: Seating goes hand in hand with menu selection. My mother-in-law never has a dinner for more than eight because she doesn't have seating for more than eight. I prefer to use two card tables set up on my lanai, so I rarely have dinner for six. The point is to choose the number of people your accommodations are best suited for. You may have to experiment to see what works best for you.

Space is an important consideration. Is there enough space for every guest to feel comfortable? Is there enough elbow room? For example, some tables for six do not accommodate six comfortably but do nicely for four. In that case, if serving dinner for eight, convert the table into a buffet and seat your guests at card tables.

Lighting: Lighting is a subtle, though important, element in the success of a dinner party. Candles are classic enhancers—nothing can bring more warmth, ease, and elegance to a party. Any candle will do, although it helps to choose ones that complement your decor and that are in scale with your table. If you've purchased new candles, do light the wicks and blow them out before your guests arrive. You don't want the shiny, new look on a candle wick.

Consider what other lighting will supplement the candles. If you have a chandelier, use it, preferably dimmed. If you don't have a chandelier, perhaps there is a lamp in the corner that will provide enough illumination. A useful tip for achieving a satisfying lighting effect is to have a triangle of lighting in a room. This seems to work most of the time and avoids glaring, overhead lights.

Decor: Decor can dictate the degree of formality or casualness of the evening. For example, a red-and-white checkered cloth with white porcelain dinnerware and stainless flatware sets a different tone from a white linen cloth with china, crystal, and sterling silver. A blue-and-white checkered cloth set with pewter falls somewhere between the two.

The most important point is to be consistent. Don't use your sterling silver with vinyl placemats. Use your silver with a white cloth (or other appropriate cloth) or individual placemats made of fabric or woven material. Your choice of tablecloth or placemats should depend upon your table and your personal preference. If you have a lovely wood or glass table, use placemats. If you're using card tables or if your table lacks graciousness, use a cloth.

Every table needs a centerpiece. There are only two helpful rules about centerpieces. The first is that they should be in scale with the table. Obviously, an 18-inch length bouquet will swallow a card table, and a small nosegay will be lost on a table seating eight. The second rule is that every centerpiece should be low enough to allow eye contact to occur across the table. This permits the conversation to flow easily across and around the table without any guest having to part the branches and peer through a centerpiece. So do be sure to measure your table area (making some allowance for serving pieces like salt and pepper shakers and cream and sugar sets) so that you can determine the ideal size for your centerpiece.

Personally, I think it's helpful to find three centerpiece options that work for you and stay with them. Here are some possibilities: an arrangement of seashells; a low-slung, green plant in a ceramic container; a tureen or special bowl or platter in which you can float gardenias or arrange other flowers; porcelain figurines; ceramic or brass fish or animals; a basket with flowers; and many more. Be sure you make a careful inventory of accessories you already own—you'll be surprised at the interesting combinations you can devise from familiar (often neglected) objects. And remember, fresh flowers that pick up and extend the color scheme you have created with your choice of tablecloth or placemats are always lovely.

In addition to the table, if you're serving a buffet, consider placing some accessory there, too. However, since the presentation of the food should be the focus, a single item will do—something that will complement the presentation of the food, not detract from it. Some ideas are a special, potted plant, a candle, a statue, a piñata if you're serving Mexican food—almost anything will do.

Music: Music, like candles, is an important mood-maker. The main thing to keep in mind when selecting your music is that it is background for good conversation; therefore, play it softly regardless of what it is. Instrumental selections tend to be better as background than vocal selections. And whether your preference be country, jazz, soft rock, big band, Spanish, or classical, try to select something peppy which adds vigor to the gathering. For example, Mozart has an "up" beat, while the blues are too melancholy. In short, select happy music for a happy occasion.

The Wines

Richard Dean is a Master Sommelier and that is no easy feat. "Sommelier" is the French term for wine steward, and the Master Sommelier title is reserved exclusively for those who have passed the rigorous examination given by the Guild of Sommeliers and the Masters of Wine in London. The third and final phase of the examination is an exclusive wine tasting party in which the examinee must eye, smell, and taste six different wines and identify the country, district, grape varietal, and vintage. "This wine is from France coming from the Burgundy (Côte de Nuits) district; the grape is pinot noir, and I would judge the vintage to be 1961." You can understand why there were only thirty Master Sommeliers in the world when Richard passed in 1975, and only three in the United States.

For the past nine years, Richard has been the sommelier at The Third Floor Restaurant in the Hawaiian Regent Hotel, one of the three best restaurants in Honolulu, we think. Richard graciously consented to match the foods of each menu in this section with a wine. Naturally a wine could be served to complement each course, and it would not be difficult to find the perfect wine for each dish if price were no object. However, since most Americans have cocktails before dinner and limited budgets, Richard confined his selection of wine for each menu to one. (Rather than cocktails, Europeans have aperitifs, such as dry vermouth, sherry, or white wine, which stimulate the appetite, not kill it.) In so doing, he considered availability and price. His guiding concept was "taste for value." Each suggested wine in its respective category represents a good bargain.

Richard suggests that all of the recommended wines in these menus, even the few reds, be served slightly chilled, and when purchasing the wine, choose the more recent vintage. For amount, there are approximately six glasses of wine in a bottle.

We trust you will enjoy the wines that accompany the menus. Undoubtedly, you will discover some personal treasures.

Island Delight for Four

Crudités with Cheese Dip

Green Salad

Island Curry

White Rice

Hot Rolls

Baked Pineapple with Chilled Custard Sauce*

Gewürztraminer, Almadén (California)

There are several important preparations you can complete early in the day before you serve this dinner. First, wash and cut your raw vegetables, such as cauliflower flowerets, cherry tomatoes, carrot sticks, and celery. Keep the carrots, celery, and cauliflower refrigerated in cold water until ready for use. Next, make the green salad of your choice and refrigerate that.

The curry will be a snap, too, if you prepare it up to the point of adding the fish. Another coup is to prepare the pineapple for baking, cover it with foil, and refrigerate. Make the custard sauce and pour into serving dish and refrigerate also.

For final assembly, pour a bottled Roquefort or bleu cheese dip into an attractive dish with your drained raw vegetables surrounding it. Reheat the curry and complete the cooking according to the directions in the recipe. About thirty minutes before dinner, begin the white rice, and fifteen minutes before serving pop some bakery-fresh rolls into the oven. After dinner, bake the pineapple immediately and serve with your Chilled Custard Sauce.

And don't forget one of the most important touches for a successful curry—the condiments. Arrange an assortment of condiments, such as shredded coconut, raisins, bacon bits, and, most essential of all, chutney, on a nice lazy susan or in individual bowls.

Although the recipe for Island Curry is for four, it can easily be doubled for a crowd of eight. If you should double the recipe, be sure to double your rice and to allow about forty minutes for the rice to cook on low.

Baked Pineapple with Chilled Custard Sauce

Pineapple*   1 or
    Pineapple chunks   two 20-ounce cans plus one 8-ounce can
        unsweetened, drained
Sugar   2 tablespoons
Rum   2 tablespoons or
    Rum extract   1 teaspoon
Butter   3 tablespoons
Strawberries, fresh mint, or maraschino cherries   garnish
Chilled Custard Sauce

Slice pineapple lengthwise just from right side of greenery. Carefully scoop out pineapple, cutting in chunks, and discard core. Be particularly careful not to cut through half with greenery still attached, for that may be used as a serving boat. Place chunks in large bowl and sprinkle with sugar and rum. Toss lightly and place in pineapple boat or in 8-inch square glass baking dish. Dot with butter, cover tightly, and refrigerate. When ready, bake uncovered at 350° for 15 to 20 minutes, or microwave at 100% for 5 minutes. Garnish with whole unhulled strawberries, fresh mint leaves, or maraschino cherries. Serve hot with sauce. Serves 8.
* To select a ripe pineapple, smell the bottom for a sweet aroma.

Chilled Custard Sauce

Egg yolks 3
Vanilla ½ teaspoon
Sugar ¼ cup
Salt ¼ teaspoon
Cornstarch 1 tablespoon
Water ¼ cup, to dissolve cornstarch
Light cream or half-and-half 2 cups
Rum 1 tablespoon

Beat yolks with vanilla and set aside. In top of double boiler pour in sugar, salt, and cornstarch that has been dissolved in water. Add cream and rum, stirring constantly over medium to medium-heat. When mixture is thoroughly heated, stir 4 tablespoons of warmed sauce into yolks. Gradually add yolk mixture to sauce and cook over hot, but not boiling, water for 3 to 4 minutes. Chill. Serve over hot baked pineapple. Makes 2 cups.

Trout Dinner for Four

Trout Grenobloise

Baked Potatoes

Sautéed Green Beans*

French Rolls

Strawberries Romanoff*

Muscadet, Loire Valley (France)

This dinner requires little effort except at the very last minute. The trout is prepared according to the recipe (do cut and decorate the lemon slices earlier in the day). In addition, trim and cut the green beans earlier in the day, patting them dry, and prepare the strawberries.

Please prepare the baked potatoes in the oven, rather than the microwave, so that the skins are crisp. Country-fried potatoes are excellent with the trout, but they require more last minute effort than I'm usually willing to give. Heat the rolls when you begin the trout.

To serve, use an oval platter, preferably high quality stainless, pewter, or silver. If it's stainless, heat it. Arrange the four trout in the center, and on one end place the hot baked potatoes. Split them open and pop in a sprig of parsley for color. If you know your guests' preferences, you can go ahead and butter or sour cream them with bacon bits and chives. Yes, do have sour cream, bacon bits, and chives available! On the other end of the platter, arrange the Sautéed Green Beans. Have different serving utensils for each. Before your guests arrive, parboil the green beans and pat them dry. Then the last five minutes you are cooking the trout, sauté the beans simultaneously. This is not difficult if you have your seasonings ready.

Sautéed Green Beans

Fresh green beans   1 pound, trimmed and cut in half
Water   enough to parboil
Butter   2 to 3 tablespoons
Salt   to taste
Beau monde   ½ teaspoon
Garlic clove   1, minced

Bring water to a boil, put in trimmed beans and parboil, uncovered, for 3 to 5 minutes. Drain and pat dry. In skillet melt butter, add garlic, and sauté for about 30 seconds. Add beans and toss. Sprinkle with salt and beau monde seasoning and sauté quickly over medium-high heat, stirring frequently, for about 3 to 5 minutes, or until tender but not limp. Serve immediately. Serves 4.
Note: To retain the rich color of vegetables, always begin cooking in boiling water, reduce heat after you place in pan.

Strawberries Romanoff

Michel, of Chez Michel's French Restaurant, kindly shared his highly praised version of this famous dessert originally created for the House of Romanoff. He suggests letting the ice cream begin to melt when you start dinner and assembling the dessert just before serving. You may prepare the berries and whipped cream in advance.

Strawberries 12, stemmed and, if large, halved
Sugar to coat berries
Bols Maraschino Liqueur ¼ cup
De Kuyper Kirschwasser ¼ cup
Cointreau 2 tablespoons
Whipping cream 2 scoops, whipped
Vanilla ice cream 2 scoops of the *real* thing
Fresh mint garnish

Sprinkle cleaned and stemmed berries with sugar, toss, and pour liqueurs over them. Toss again, being careful not to bruise berries. Cover and refrigerate. Whip cream early in day and refrigerate. Allow ice cream to melt at room temperature in large bowl. Fold whipped cream into melted ice cream, then fold in berry mixture. Place dollops of dessert into individual compotes or champagne glasses, decorate with a sprig of mint, and refrigerate. Serves 4.

Uncle Jack's Southern Dinner for Four

Southern Deep-Fried Sauger

Baked Cheese Grits*

Coleslaw

Chilled Sliced Tomatoes

Hush Puppies

Sumptuous Peach Ice Cream*

Muffin Brownies

Chablis, Paul Masson (California)

This is the dinner served by my aunt and uncle described in the recipe for the sauger. Of course, you can use other fish. Choose your own favorite coleslaw recipe and make that early in the day and slice and chill the tomatoes. Make the brownies in a muffin pan and set those aside. Beware of nibbling—they're very good.

Make the batter for the hush puppies according to the directions on the packaged mix or recipe of your choice and cook in the same oil in which you fry the fish.

The peach ice cream is made in an ice cream freezer—my aunt and uncle make it right on the dock.

This is the kind of dinner that makes you want to show up with all your kids, and everyone relaxes and visits.

Baked Cheese Grits

Quick grits 1 cup
Boiling water 4 cups
Salt 1 teaspoon
Tillamook sharp cheese 6 ounces, diced and shredded
Butter ½ cup
Milk ½ cup
Eggs 2, well beaten
Parsley-Garlic Mix (see Index) 1 teaspoon

Pour grits into boiling water and add salt. Cook 3 to 5 minutes, stirring occasionally. Stir in remaining ingredients and cook over low heat until cheese melts. Grease a 2-quart casserole and pour in grit mixture. Bake at 350° for 1 hour. Serves 6 to 8.

Sumptuous Peach Ice Cream

Fresh peaches 4 cups, peeled and mashed
Sugar 3½ cups
Whipping cream 2 cups
Lemon juice from 1
Salt dash
Vanilla ¾ teaspoon
Half-and-half enough to fill ice cream maker can ¾ full

Mix all ingredients except half-and-half and toss gently so as not to damage peaches. Put mixture into ice cream cannister and fill to ¾ full with half-and-half. Proceed according to directions for your machine. Makes 2½ to 3 quarts.

Sturgeon Feast for Four

Grilled Sturgeon with Mushroom Sauce

Asparagus and Broccoli Vinaigrette*

Fluffy Mashed Potatoes*

Chilled Mandarin Oranges with Kirschwasser

Butter Cookies

Chardonnay, Château Ste. Michelle (Washington)

Marvelous news! The asparagus and broccoli, the mashed potatoes, the mushroom sauce, and the mandarin oranges are prepared in advance. Thus, the evening you are entertaining, you have only to warm the sauce and the potatoes and cook the sturgeon. Naturally you may substitute another fish for the sturgeon, such as halibut or mahimahi, but if you can obtain sturgeon, do it!

To prepare the mandarin oranges, buy the cans available in the market. Drain them and, reserving the syrup, place them in individual champagne glasses. Sprinkle them with chopped pecans. Mix an ounce or two of the syrup with an equal amount of kirschwasser and pour over each serving. Cover and chill for several hours. Before serving, lightly toss each one and garnish with fresh mint.

You may make the fluffy mashed potatoes as early as three days in advance; just cover well and refrigerate. The salad of asparagus and broccoli may also be made the day before. All of this advance preparation permits you to give your undivided attention to the sturgeon. Watch it, baste it, and it will be divine!

Asparagus and Broccoli Vinaigrette

Broccoli   1 large bunch or 2 smaller ones
White asparagus spears   two 2-ounce cans, drained
Vinaigrette dressing   to cover, homemade or bottled
Cherry tomatoes   1 basket, rinsed and dried
Hard-cooked egg yolk   garnish

Trim heavy stems from broccoli, leaving primarily bouquets. Bring salted water to a boil, add broccoli bouquets, and cook uncovered for 8 minutes (also 8 minutes in microwave). Drain and cool. Marinate broccoli and asparagus in vinaigrette dressing for several hours in refrigerator, turning occasionally. Add rinsed, dried tomatoes during last 30 minutes of marinating time. Roll gently in dressing. One hour before serving, gently lift asparagus from marinade and place attractively in center of small platter. Ring asparagus with drained cherry tomatoes and broccoli bouquets. Cover and refrigerate until ready to serve. Sprinkle minced egg yolk over asparagus just before serving. Serve immediately. Serves 6.

Fluffy Mashed Potatoes

Potatoes   8 to 10, peeled and chunked
Sour cream   1 cup
Cream cheese   8-ounce package
Garlic cloves   2, pressed
Salt   1 teaspoon
White pepper   ½ teaspoon
Butter   1 tablespoon
Paprika   garnish

Cook peeled and chunked potatoes in lightly salted water until very tender and drain. Meanwhile beat sour cream, cream cheese, garlic, salt, and pepper on medium speed until well blended. Set aside. Return potatoes to pan (unless teflon, in which case use something else). Gradually beat in sour cream mixture, breaking up potatoes. When most big lumps are gone, turn beater to high and beat until all lumps are gone and potatoes are smooth and creamy. Pour into a 2-quart casserole. Dot with butter and sprinkle with paprika. You may cover and refrigerate at this point. If not refrigerated, bake at 325° for 20 minutes; if refrigerated, bake for 40 to 45 minutes.
Note: I've rarely had leftovers, nor has my Aunt Camille before me, and when I do, I make potato cakes.

Elegant Kumu and Kasha for Six

Boiled Ham Rolls

Artichokes with Mayonnaise

Oven-Steamed Kumu with Capers and Wine

Kasha

Quartered Mushrooms*

Breadsticks

Summer Melon Bowl

Vanilla Sauce*

Fumé Blanc, Robert Mondavi (California)

A whole fish served attractively is a masterful stroke in subtle elegance. I admit my prejudice. If I could, I would serve this for every major dinner of any consequence.

The boiled ham rolls and the artichokes are served with cocktails or predinner beverages. The day before, cook the artichokes (about two or three) in hot water sprinkled with oil and with two chopped garlic cloves tossed in. Drain and chill them. When cool, trim them, laying a lemon slice across the top. Flavor the mayonnaise with herbs if you wish. For the boiled ham rolls, purchase a small package of boiled ham (Danish is fine), and cut the slices into quarters. Meanwhile either purchase a small cheese herb spread, or mix some tarragon with cream cheese and let it blend flavors overnight. Spread each quarter of ham with the cheese, and then roll up the ham. Arrange the rolls attractively the day of the party; you might arrange them around the artichokes or on a separate tray with doily or bed of watercress or parsley. (Do remember a dish for discarded artichoke leaves.)

For the kasha, cook according to the directions on the package that indicate using chicken broth and sautéing onions. You may find kasha, which is buckwheat groats, in the gourmet section of the market or in the rice section. If you can't find kasha, then try cracked wheat bulgur (also with onions and chicken broth), and if you can't find that, settle for pilaf. Allow about 5 to 10 minutes longer to cook than stated on the boxes.

The mushrooms may be cut earlier in the day and stored in a plastic bag in the refrigerator. Do make the Parsley-Garlic Mix ahead of time;

you don't want to be doing that with company present.

The melon bowl is a wonderful dessert in the summer months. Go for the colorful selections—honeydew, watermelon, and canteloupe. Use a melon baller which, with a whip of the wrist, creates a perfect ball. Put this together in the afternoon with one important warning—if you make the melon bowl too early, you will have to pour out the accumulated juices. Serve it in a glass bowl with the Vanilla Sauce on the side. Lemon meringue pie or Iced Lemon Tortoni Pie (see Index) may be substituted for melons and sauce.

Quartered Mushrooms

Butter   2½ tablespoons
Mushrooms   3 cups, quartered
Parsley-Garlic Mix   2 tablespoons

Melt 2 tablespoons butter in frying pan and sauté mushrooms over medium-high heat. When butter is absorbed, add remaining ½ tablespoon butter and sauté until melted. Set aside until just before serving. When ready, reheat mushrooms and add Parsley-Garlic Mix. Sauté over high heat until heated through. Serve immediately. Serves 4.

Parsley-Garlic Mix

Parsley   1 bunch
Garlic cloves   4

Combine parsley and garlic in food processor or blender and mix until both are minced and well blended. Cover and refrigerate. Makes 1 cup. **Note:**   If you're not a garlic lover, reduce the number of cloves to 2. I use this mix in sautéing mushrooms, baking tomatoes, sautéing chicken livers, etc. Consequently, I usually have some on hand in the refrigerator, well covered, of course.

Vanilla Sauce

Sugar ¼ cup
Cornstarch 1 tablespoon
Water 1 cup
Butter 2 tablespoons
Ground lemon peel ⅛ teaspoon
Vanilla 2 teaspoons

Combine sugar, cornstarch, and water in double boiler and heat over hot water until thickened, stirring constantly. Remove from heat and add remaining ingredients. Stir well. Cool, pour into serving dish, and chill. Makes 1 cup.
Variation: Add 1 tablespoon fresh lemon juice or lime juice if you prefer a sauce that's more tart than sweet.

Sole Dinner for Six

Celeriac Salad*

Fillets of Sole Meunière

Potatoes Anna*

Chilled Sliced Tomatoes

Fresh Nectarine Pie*

Piesporter Goldtröpfchen, Havemeyer (Germany)

This is a lovely dinner for six, and again, most of the dishes are made in advance. Make the pie the day before. That morning prepare the celeriac salad and slice the large, ripe tomatoes. Measure and combine the bread crumb mixture for the sole, cover, and set aside. Also prepare the garnishes. Get out the serving dishes or trays and set the table. I prefer a more elegant setting; it compliments the simplicity of the meal. Candles are a must, as always! I serve the Celeriac Salad on a bed of lettuce on individual salad plates as a first course; otherwise, the Cajun Sauce would overwhelm the delicate sole. However, the salad may also be served buffet-style; just chill it in an attractive mold.

I serve the Potatoes Anna on a round silver tray and garnish them with minced parsley. To serve, just slice as you would a pie. Also garnish the tomatoes with minced parsley, and sprinkle with a dash of salt. The sole fillets are lovely served on a silver tray surrounded with lemon wedges or slices and clumps of parsley.

Celeriac Salad

This salad is one of my favorites. It's different and everyone seems to love it. Best of all, it is made ahead of time! I have served the celeriac cubed, julienned, and thinly sliced. I think I prefer the latter, and I use the food processor for slicing.

Cajun Sauce (see Index)   ½ cup
Chicken bouillon cubes   2
Hot water   2 cups
Lemon juice   2 tablespoons
Celeriac   1 very large or 2 medium, peeled, trimmed, and thinly sliced
Leeks   2, white portions only, thinly sliced
Salt   ¼ teaspoon
Parsley   2 tablespoons finely chopped
Pimientos   1 tablespoon chopped

Make sauce and set aside at room temperature. Dissolve bouillon cubes in hot water, add lemon juice, and set aside. Peel, trim, and slice celeriac. In a shallow dish microwave celeriac in chicken broth for 8 minutes at 100%. (Or bring to boil and simmer on stove for 10 minutes.) Meanwhile slice white portions of leeks and continue slicing partially into green. Add leeks, salt, and parsley to celeriac and microwave another 8 minutes at 100% or simmer for another 10 minutes on stove. Drain and cool. Toss with chopped pimientos and sauce. Chill thoroughly for at least 2 hours. Serves 6.

Potatoes Anna

The food processor does a terrific job on slicing the potatoes as thin as they should be. When arranging the potatoes in the pie plate, heap the center a little higher than the sides because in cooking, the center may fall somewhat.

Medium potatoes   6, peeled and thinly sliced
Butter   6 tablespoons, melted
Onion   1 tablespoon diced
Parsley   1 tablespoon chopped
Gruyère cheese   2 tablespoons grated (optional)
Parsley   garnish

Place potato slices immediately in ice water and soak for 30 minutes. Drain and pat dry with paper towels. Layer slices in buttered glass pie plate. Pour 1 tablespoon melted butter over first layer and dribble ⅓ onions, parsley, and cheese over layer. Continue layering potatoes, pouring a little butter over layers and sprinkling with onions, parsley, and cheese until all are used up. Do not use more than 6 tablespoons butter or potatoes will not brown. Save some butter to pour over top. Bake in preheated 450° oven for 45 minutes, or until potatoes are soft. Invert on serving tray and sprinkle with chopped parsley. Serves 6.

Fresh Nectarine Pie

Nectarines   6 cups peeled and sliced
Sugar   1 cup
Cornstarch   3 tablespoons
Orange juice   ½ cup
Lemon juice   2 tablespoons
Vanilla   ¼ teaspoon
Pie crust   9-inch baked pie shell
Nectarine slices, fresh mint, or whole strawberries   garnish

Mash 1 cup of nectarines and set rest aside. In saucepan blend sugar and cornstarch and stir in orange juice and 1 cup mashed fruit. Cook over medium heat, stirring constantly, until mixture thickens and boils, about 8 minutes. Boil and stir for 1 minute. Remove pan from heat and stir in lemon juice and vanilla. Cool. Pour ½ glaze mixture into baked pie shell. Spread mixture over bottom and sides, being certain to completely cover pie shell. Fill with remaining 5 cups of sliced nectarines. Top pie with remaining ½ glaze. Refrigerate for at least 3 hours. Garnish with circle of nectarine slices glazed in sugar water, or simply use mint or strawberries. Serve well chilled. Serves 6.

Sheldon Zane's French Feast for Six

Poached Oysters in Spinach Leaves

Crab with Mousseline Sauce in Ramekins

Fresh Maine Lobster with Tarragon Butter Sauce

Cheese and Fruit

Sorbet de Pamplemousse*

Chardonnay, Beringer (California)

This is indeed a feast for the gods, particularly Aphrodite. Although we've recommended the Beringer Chardonnay, here's the lineup of more expensive California wines that Sheldon and Gwen Zane served with this meal: Domaine Chandon Brut before dinner; St. Jean Chardonnay 1976 with the oysters; Château Montelena Chardonnay 1975 with the crab; Charles Le Franc Johannisberg Riesling 1976 with the lobster; and Warres Oporto 1962 after dessert. But remember, your meal will be heavenly no matter which wines you choose to serve.

Although you can certainly make the meal more spectacular by preparing all the dishes while your guests are sipping their wine, you may feel more relaxed if you've prepared certain dishes in advance. For example, you might have the oysters made to the point of placing them on the stove and the crab to the point stated in the recipe. In the late afternoon, you might split and clean the lobster and prepare the tarragon butter sauce.

An assortment of fruits and cheeses follows the lobster. Bel Paese, Camembert, Brie, Gruyère, and Cheddar are a few of the cheeses I would recommend, and apples and pears fruits that are delightful accompaniments to these.

Of course, the sorbet must be made in advance. Gwen says the grapefruit cleanses the palate and is a nice final addition to a seafood feast. Champagne or sherbet glasses work very well.

Have all garnishes cut, chopped, or trimmed and placed in plastic bags. Parsley shows off the lobster well. The oysters are particularly attractive when served on special salad plates, such as old ones that you may have accumulated in your family. The crab ramekins are placed on individual plates, and lemon wedges with a small twig of parsley look very nice alongside.

All in all, it will be a night to remember.

Sorbet de Pamplemousse

Sugar   1 cup
Water   2 cups
Fresh grapefruit juice   1 cup
Crème de cassis   (optional)
Fresh mint   garnish

Bring sugar and water to boil until sugar dissolves. Stir in juice and liqueur and freeze in ice cream machine. Serve in individual champagne or sherbet glasses topped with a sprig of mint. Serves 6.

Polynesian Barbecue for Six

Polynesian Steelhead BBQ

Cucumbers with Sour Cream*

Country-Fried Potatoes

Hot Blackberry Pie à la Mode

Johannisberg Riesling, Château Ste. Michelle (Washington State)

Although the recipe is for steelhead, salmon would do equally well. This is another easy dinner for entertaining. Marinate the steaks ahead of time, even the day before, and make the cucumber salad the morning of your dinner. You may either make your own pie or buy it from a bakery. To fry the potatoes, cut extra large french fries from the whole potato. You may cut these earlier and cover them in cold water, adding salt and a little sugar so they will not discolor. Drain them, pat dry, and deep fry in an oil suitable for high heat.

This is definitely a meal with "informal" written all over it.

Cucumbers with Sour Cream

Large cucumbers   3, peeled and thinly sliced
Salt   ½ teaspoon
White wine vinegar   3 tablespoons
Water   3 tablespoons
Sugar   1 teaspoon
White pepper   ⅛ teaspoon
Beau monde   ⅛ teaspoon
Sour cream   ¾ cup
Fresh dill or fresh watercress tips   garnish

Peel cucumbers and slice by hand or in a food processor. Salt, cover, and weight slices, and chill for at least 1 hour. Press out accumulated liquid. Combine vinegar, water, sugar, pepper, and beau monde with cucumber and fold in sour cream. Sprinkle top with dill. (If making ahead of time, don't add sour cream until late in afternoon, and again, press out juices before doing so.) Serves 6.

Fruit 'n' Fish Dinner for Six

Chinese Pea Pod Salad with Fruit Slices*

Honey Fruit Dressing*

Mahimahi-Halibut Supreme

Potatoes Anna

Vanilla Ice Cream

Grandmother Adams's Chocolate Sauce*

Sauvignon Blanc, Buena Vista (California)

This casual meal is colorful, well balanced, and wholesome. It's also easy to prepare. During the day, prepare the salad without the dressing. Cover and refrigerate. You may also make the chocolate sauce and refrigerate.

Slice the tomatoes for the Mahimahi-Halibut Supreme; grate or dice the Swiss cheese and make the Parsley-Garlic Mix. Mince the dill, also, if you're using it. Mix the curry powder with the mayonnaise and refrigerate. For six people, use about 4 tablespoons of mayonnaise to 1 teaspoon of curry powder. The fish steaks should be about ½-inch thick and weigh about .35 to .42 pounds each. In cooking six steaks, the microwave time will increase slightly. After the 4 minutes called for in the recipe, turn the steaks so that the inside portions are now the outside portions and microwave for another 2 minutes.

If you wish, you may substitute rice pilaf for the Potatoes Anna.

Reheat the chocolate sauce just before serving; it should be just warmed.

Chinese Pea Pod Salad with Fruit Slices

This refreshing salad complements seafood well. Do try to obtain the smaller pea pods as you want them tender and crunchy!

Fresh Chinese pea pods   ½ pound, preferably young
Ruby grapefruit   1, peeled and in wedges with most pulp removed
Oranges   3, peeled and in wedges with most pulp removed
Honey Fruit Dressing
Watercress or lettuce   1 bunch
Radishes or cherry tomatoes   garnish

Rinse and trim ends of pea pods. Peel and prepare fruit wedges. Place bed of watercress on individual salad plates. Upon each, arrange about 7 pea pods on left side and alternate 3 orange wedges with 2 grapefruit wedges on right side of plate. Place rose-cut radish below pea pods and near fruit. Spoon dressing over salad and serve immediately. Serves 6.

Honey Fruit Dressing

Jean Hindman gives lovely luncheons, and I always come home with one of her special recipes. In this instance, it was her dressing for a fruit salad.

Sugar   ⅔ cup
Dry mustard   1 teaspoon
Paprika   1 teaspoon
Salt   1 teaspoon
Onion powder   1 teaspoon
Celery seed   1 teaspoon
Honey   ½ cup
Lemon rind   1 teaspon grated or minced
White wine vinegar   ¼ cup
Pimientos   1 teaspoon diced
Salad oil   1 cup

Combine all ingredients except oil. Gradually beat in oil with wire whisk. If refrigerated, dressing becomes very thick, so remove it from refrigerator and let sit at room temperature for a while before serving over salad. Makes 2½ cups.
Note: This dressing makes a sizable amount, but you can use the extra for other fruit salads.

Grandmother Adams's Chocolate Sauce*

Some of my fondest memories are of my grandmother's kitchen. What a country cook! Little did we know as children that she had risen at dawn to tend her chickens and weed her large garden, although I often remember her in her sunbonnet, hoeing long rows of beans. She was always busy with the basics of living. Yet at 6:30 p.m., when she had been off her feet for only fifteen minutes, we would plead for popcorn balls or chocolate sauce, and she and Aunt Bernice would get up and make it. Not a word of complaint, not a sigh, just a low, gentle chuckle.

Sugar   1½ cups
Cocoa   3 tablespoons
Milk   ½ cup
Vanilla   ⅛ teaspoon

Stir sugar and cocoa together in saucepan. Add milk, stir, and add vanilla and stir again. Bring mixture to a boil, stirring constantly, for about 4 to 5 minutes or until sauce is thickened and drips from spoon. Makes 1⅓ cups.
* If refrigerated, this sauce thickens and takes a long, low heat with a little

milk (or a double boiler) to return it to the proper consistency. It is best served warm immediately after making.

Mediterranean Dinner for Six

Assorted Cheeses

Marinated Artichoke Hearts and Brussels Sprouts

Tabouleh Salad*

Bass Baked in Greek Bouillabaisse Sauce

Rice Pilaf

Sautéed Zucchini Cubes

Baklava

Chenin Blanc, Charles Krug (California)

This is a casual evening for good friends, Greek music, and laughter. You can even dance if you wish. Begin the evening with assorted cheeses, such as feta, Camembert, or Brie, or other favorite selections. Serve cheese with Armenian rye crackers and have small trays of marinated artichoke hearts and brussels sprouts available with toothpicks and napkins.

The first course is the Tabouleh Salad. You may assemble this in advance up to the point of mashing the onion and adding the dressing.

For additional convenience, you can purchase packaged rice pilaf. Or you can make you own by sautéing long-grain rice in butter until barely golden. Stir in boiling chicken broth, cover, and simmer on low for about forty minutes. For six people use about 2 cups of rice to 3¾ cups of chicken broth.

Check your Yellow Pages for a Mediterranean or Middle Eastern bakery that makes baklava, an absolutely divine dessert, but tortuous to make. You can also call your local Greek society to help you locate this fabulous pastry, or call any restaurant that is even near the Middle East in its cuisine. Order it in advance for pick-up the day of the party (or day before if absolutely necessary). If you are obtaining it from a bakery or restaurant, inquire about an appropriate bread, such as Armenian lavosh. If you're unable to find an appropriate bread, then settle for fresh, crusty French bread with room-temperature butter. If you're unable to find baklava, settle for the Iced Lemon Tortoni Pie (see Index), or sherbet, whatever your druthers are.

You can make the Bouillabaisse Sauce the day before; in fact, it will be more flavorful if you do. In the afternoon of the appointed day, slice the tomato slices for the fish, blend the Parsley-Garlic Mix, and toss the bread crumbs with melted butter; do keep the bread crumbs at room temperature. You may also do any chopping or dicing necessary for the Tabouleh Salad, prepare the chicken broth or bouillon cubes for the pilaf, and cube the zucchini for sautéing.

To sauté the zucchini, melt some butter in a frying pan and add a handful of chopped onions. Cook until translucent, add zucchini, salt and white pepper to taste, and sauté very quickly over medium-high heat. Add a dash of nutmeg for extra flavor. Don't overcook.

A time scenario might look like this:

6:00   Marinate fish steaks and arrange cheese and marinated vegetables.
6:30   Preheat oven when you hear doorbell; serve cocktails and hors d'oeuvres.
6:45   Put on pilaf.
7:00   Pour sauce over fish and put in oven; serve Tabouleh Salad.
7:20   Check on fish; it may take a few minutes longer since sauce was cold; sauté zucchini.
7:30   Serve entrée.

After dinner serve the baklava with coffee; espresso or Turkish coffee would be ideal.

Tabouleh Salad

Marion Gedeon, recently arrived from Lebanon, prepares a superb, crunchy Tabouleh Salad. She prefers the wild Chinese parsley if you happen upon it, and she prefers the crunchy bulgur to the soaked. A Middle East bakery will carry the crunchy variety, and if you're unable to locate a Middle East bakery, she suggests you use Ala bulgur unsoaked.

Chinese parsley   6 bunches, chopped
Medium tomatoes   2, diced
Bulgur wheat   ½ to ¾ cup
Dried mint   1 teaspoon
Small onion   1, diced
Salt   1 teaspoon
Old Spice*   ¼ teaspoon
Lemon   juice from 1
Olive oil   ½ cup

In an attractive bowl layer parsley, tomatoes, and bulgur topped with mint. Before serving, mash onion with salt and Old Spice and mix with lemon juice. Gradually whip in olive oil. Pour over salad and leave as is or toss. Serves 6.

* This spice contains pepper.

Elegant Pasta for Six

Antipasto

Tossed Green Salad

Scampi with Fettucine

French Bread (optional)

Vanilla Ice Cream with Berries

Soave, Bolla (Italy)

Have the antipasto ready to assemble just before your guests arrive. Cover a large platter with a bed of lettuce or watercress, and artistically arrange an assortment of foods, such as Tuscan peppers (they come in a jar near the pickles), sliced salami and/or ham, black olives and stuffed green olives, cheese, cherry tomatoes, deviled eggs, and definitely pickled vegetables (also in jars near the pickles). Serve the antipasto as hors d'oeuvres with cocktails or other predinner beverages.

Have your green salad made in advance except for adding the sliced tomatoes and the oil and vinegar dressing. Toss just before serving.

To prepare the Scampi with Fettucine ahead of time, refer to the note following that recipe.

The French bread is optional, but if served, should be crusty and fresh and served with room-temperature butter.

The ice cream (and yes, *real* ice cream) with berries should be served in compotes. Any choice of berries will do, but if fresh, be sure you rinsed and sugared them earlier in the day, and if frozen, do remember to thaw them. Oh hideous thought!

Service-wise, this meal is better suited to the hostess's serving at the table (thereby assuring everyone gets the same amount of shrimp), or as my mother-in-law does, serve it in the kitchen.

Elegant Dining for Eight

Spinach Salad

Sole with Shrimp Sauce au Gratin

Pilaf

Baked Tomatoes

Hot Rolls

Chilled Lemon Tarts

Johannisberg Riesling, Robert Mondavi (California)

This is a marvelous dinner for entertaining, not only in taste, but because everything but the pilaf may be made ahead of time and refrigerated.

Make the spinach salad and refrigerate, but don't add the vinaigrette dressing until the last minute, and don't have any tomatoes in the salad.

Make the sole early that morning according to the recipe. Obtain large tomatoes (hothouse variety is very nice in the winter), and make nice thick slices. Sprinkle the tomatoes with the Parsley-Garlic Mix (see Index). Top with bread crumbs mixed with a little melted butter, cover, and refrigerate.

Either buy a packaged pilaf or use your own favorite recipe. Lazy as I am, I also purchase the chilled lemon tarts from a bakery, and if the tarts are not available, I substitute a lemon meringue pie or Iced Lemon Tortoni Pie (see Index).

Serve the spinach salad as a first course. This means arranging the salad on individual salad plates and placing them on larger dinner plates at the individual setting. Now quickly pop the sole and the rolls into the preheated oven for seven minutes. For heaven's sake—set a timer! Now announce that dinner is served and usher your guests into the dining area. When the timer sounds, pop the tomatoes in the oven and set the timer for another eight minutes. That will be the signal that everything is done in the oven. Do watch the rolls, though, since rolls vary according to time needed for heating or browning.

Salmon Barbecue for Eight

Crispy Wun Tun

Barbecued Whole Salmon

Hostess Potatoes*

Baby Sweet Peas

Chocolate Chip Cake*

Bishop of Riesling (Germany)

This hearty dinner on a cool night would be most suitable for a neighborhood gathering. It has the added benefit of advance preparation for most dishes.

Make the Crispy Wun Tun and the Hostess Potatoes ahead of time and refrigerate. Bake the cake that morning or the day before if necessary.

Before your guests arrive, heat oven to 400° and lay wun tun on brown paper bag on cookie sheet. Reheat for ten to fifteen minutes until heated throughout. Serve when guests arrive with Chinese Dipping Sauce.

Prepare the fish for cooking and set aside in its foil wrap. For eight people you'll require at least a 5½-pound fish before cleaning, 4 pounds after cleaning. When you put the salmon on the coals, pop the potatoes into the oven and set the timer. Since potatoes were refrigerated, they may require an additional five to ten minutes.

Just before fish is done, prepare the sweet peas. Serve fish whole on an attractive platter and permit guests to help themselves buffet-style.

Hostess Potatoes

Olive Brown serves this with her whole salmon and she prefers the cream of chicken soup. However, another friend serves a similar dish, and she prefers cream of mushroom soup. To confuse the issue totally, cream of celery soup would blend nicely also. Experiment—make it three times, each time with a different soup, and choose your personal favorite.

Medium potatoes   8 to 10, cooked, peeled, and grated
Condensed cream of chicken, mushroom, or celery soup
      10¾-ounce can
Sour cream   1 cup
Cheddar cheese   1¼ cups grated
Green onions   ½ cup chopped
Cornflake crumbs   to cover
Butter   ½ cup, melted

Boil, peel, and grate potatoes. Mix soup with sour cream. Add cheese and green onions. Fold into grated potatoes and pour into buttered 9 by 12-inch casserole. Top with cornflakes and pour over butter. Bake at 350° for 40 minutes. (If it has been refrigerated, allow an additional 5 to 10 minutes.) Let set for 10 minutes before serving. Serves 8 to 10.

Chocolate Chip Cake

This is another of Jean Hindman's special desserts. If I ate there often, I would weigh a ton. She says you can frost this cake if you wish, but it's rich enough without any frosting.

Noninstant chocolate pudding mix   4-ounce package
Rich chocolate cake mix   18½-ounce package (without pudding)
Chocolate chips   1 cup
Walnuts   1 cup, chopped

Make pudding according to recipe on package. Cool. Stir into cake mix and blend thoroughly. Butter or grease a bundt pan and pour in cake mixture. Sprinkle chocolate chips and nuts over top. Bake at 350° for 30 minutes or until done. Serves 10.

Casual Clamming for Eight

Linguine with White Clam Sauce

Tossed Green Salad

Crusty French Bread

Assorted Pastries

Soave, Bolla (Italy)

God bless my friend Joan for introducing me to her Linguine with White Clam Sauce! It is such an easy meal, and it's so refreshing, both on the palate and the budget. Make the bouillon in advance and add the clam juice and have your seasonings ready, so that at the last minute all you have to do is stir.

A crusty French bread is a necessity—or should I say Italian in this case? Serve it at room temperature with room-temperature butter. The salad may be made ahead, but tossed with a vinegar-oil dressing at the last minute.

Assorted pastries are a delightful closing to this meal. Select some of your favorite bakery's Napoleons, cream puffs, petit fours, etc. If you are watching the budget, perhaps you might want to substitute vanilla ice cream with a warmed chocolate sauce and shortbread cookies.

Great Gumbo for Ten

Fish and Sausage Gumbo

Cucumbers with Sour Cream

Hearty French Bread

Fruits and Cheeses

Beaujolais, Louis Jadot (France)

This is another fine dinner for entertaining because everything is made in advance, and you will need to be in the kitchen only for the last fifteen minutes before serving. Make the Fish and Sausage Gumbo according to the directions, even making a large portion of it the day before.

The Cucumbers with Sour Cream (see Index) also is made in

advance.

The hearty French bread is an absolute must! Go to a bakery (order in advance) and pick up three loaves of fresh bread with a *thick* crust, even though you will most likely only need two. Have two sticks of butter at room temperature. Set one loaf of bread and a stick of butter at one end of the table and another at the other end and allow your guests to break their own bread in the manner of the French countryside.

Select a good assortment of fruits; pears are perfect, include apples, one or two oranges or tangerines—whatever is in season. Arrange attractively in a bowl (or two bowls—one for each end of the table) and serve with several cheeses. Camembert and Brie cheeses are excellent, and you might include a hard cheese if you wish. A simple and satisfying meal!

Italian Fare for Twelve

Port Cheddar Cheese with Assorted Crackers

Calamari

Seafood Lasagna

Crusty Garlic Bread

Tossed Green Salad

Oil and Vinegar Dressing

Spumoni Ice Cream

Bardolino, Bolla (Italy)

Bring out the red-checkered tablecloth, the wine carafes, and the candles and sing a little Puccini. This Italian buffet is a hearty meal.

The only last-minute effort is to cook the Calamari, although you already have it sliced, ready to dip, roll, and sauté. The lasagna is all ready to pop into the oven, as is the garlic bread, and the tossed green salad is assembled in its serving bowl except for the tomatoes (if you include them) and dressing. The spumoni ice cream is in the freezer, and the coffee is ready to be plugged in.

You may mix the Spinach-Mushroom Mix for the lasagna the day before, grate the necessary cheeses, and definitely prepare the Italian Diablo Sauce the day prior so that the flavors may blend. This leaves only the Seafood Mix, the garlic bread, the cooking of the lasagna noodles, and the assembling to be done the day of the party.

You may even clean and slice the squid for the Calamari the day before as long as you cover it well and refrigerate.

Before your guests arrive, set out the port Cheddar with your favorite crackers and several bowls of pitted black olives. Marinated vegetables would be a suitable addition. Small hors d'oeuvre plates and napkins should be available also.

When most of your guests have arrived, cook the Calamari and serve hot.

When you remove the lasagna from the oven, pop in the bread wrapped in foil (400° for 15 minutes). Now toss the salad and place on the buffet. Next, cut the lasagna into serving portions and place on large platters (you may require several), and serve immediately with the hot bread.

Later, spumoni ice cream served with your favorite cookies or madeleines will clear the palate and pave the way for an after-dinner liqueur, such as Galliano.

A Summer Buffet for Twelve

Crudités with Spinach Dip

Caviar Classic

Salade Beatrice*

Chilled Poached Whole Salmon

Aioli Sauce

Cucumber Sauce

Green Mayonnaise

Artichoke Bottoms Crowned with Sautéed Mushrooms*

Spinach Noodles

Iced Lemon Tortoni Pie*

Vouvray, Château Moncontour (France)

This elaborate, sumptuous summer buffet offers the delight of advance preparation with every dish but the spinach noodles, and while this menu is offered as a summer dinner, it could also serve as a bountiful brunch.

Several days, or even a week before, prepare and freeze two Iced Lemon Tortoni Pies. Three days prior, make the spinach dip for the crudités, which is the Spinach-Clam Spread sans clams plus a little added mayonnaise.

Two days before, make your own French dressing, or purchase a good bottled version. You may also cook and julienne the beets this day and boil the eggs for the Salade Beatrice. Boil additional eggs if you plan to make deviled eggs as a garnish for the fish. In addition, you may make the jellied consommé today.

The day before, sauté the mushrooms, drain, and heap them in twelve canned artichoke bottoms. Place the artichoke bottoms in cooking dish with chicken stock, cover, and refrigerate.

Also make 2 cups each of the Aioli and Cucumber sauces and the Green Mayonnaise. Chill in their respective serving bowls. Cut the crudités, soaking any celery or carrots in water, and refrigerate.

The day of the party, slice tomatoes and arrange the Salade Beatrice, except for the dressing and garnish, on a silver platter. Also, gather the ingredients for the Caviar Classic and refrigerate. Finally, prepare and decorate the poached salmon.

Before your guests arrive, arrange the crudités with the spinach dip and have the water ready to cook the spinach noodles. When guests arrive, serve crudités and Caviar Classic with rye crackers, toasted melba, or sesame rounds. When ready to serve, cook the noodles and reheat the artichoke bottoms. Drain noodles and heap on platter; surround with the twelve artichoke bottoms. Serve immediately with the Salade Beatrice, poached salmon, and chilled sauces.

Salade Beatrice

Beets   4 cups cooked and julienned
French dressing   to cover
Lettuce leaves
Large tomatoes   4, sliced
Asparagus tips   three 10½-ounce cans, drained
Hard-cooked eggs   garnish
Chives   garnish

Marinate beets in dressing for 1 hour. Drain and proceed to assemble salad. On bed of lettuce leaves, arrange an outer ring of sliced tomatoes.

Next, arrange large ring of beets, and in center well arrange asparagus tips. Dribble a little dressing over vegetables and garnish with chopped eggs and finely chopped chives. Serves 12.

Artichoke Bottoms Crowned with Sautéed Mushrooms

Canned artichoke bottoms 12
Mushrooms 1½ cups, small fresh ones, thinly sliced
Butter 1 tablespoon
Chicken broth one and one-half 14½-ounce cans, enough to form ¼-inch depth

Drain and set out artichoke bottoms. Sauté mushrooms in butter and drain well. Distribute mushrooms in artichoke bottoms. Arrange artichoke bottoms in shallow 9 by 13-inch baking dish and pour in stock to cover bottom. Cover and refrigerate. When ready to serve, reheat slowly, without boiling, until mushrooms and artichoke bottoms are heated through. Arrange on platter and serve immediately. Serves 12.

Iced Lemon Tortoni Pie

This marvelous dessert clears the palate and is delightfully easy to make.

Frozen lemonade 6-ounce can, undiluted and thawed
Vanilla ice cream 1 quart, softened
Rum extract ¼ teaspoon
Graham cracker pie crust one 9-inch, baked
Fresh mint garnish
Lemon slices or strawberries garnish

Beat lemonade into ice cream, add rum extract, and pour into crust. Freeze for at least 4 hours (you can freeze up to 2 weeks). Remove from freezer so that it softens somewhat before cutting (don't allow it to soften too much). Garnish with mint leaves and lemon slices or strawberries. Serves 6.

Autumn Brunch for Four

Creamed Finnan Haddie

Toasted English Muffins

Sweet-Sour Green Beans*

Boiled Potatoes with Dill

Pumpkin Pie

Monterey Riesling, Mirassou (California)

By doubling the finnan haddie recipe you will have an easy brunch for eight. Make the finnan haddie in advance, even the day before, for it reheats well in a microwave at 50%, stirring frequently, or on the stove or in a chafing dish. Reheat first, though, before you put it in a chafing dish.

The Sweet-Sour Green Beans are also made the day before; in fact, they require marinating overnight, so they only need to be reheated.

Before your guests arrive, split the muffins and butter them and later pop them under the broiler to lightly brown. Do set a timer! (I'm always forgetting foods in the broiler.) Have the potatoes cooking when your guests arrive, to be finished at the appointed time you plan to serve the brunch. Drain the potatoes quickly while they are still steaming and immediately pour them back into the hot pan. Set the pan over high heat and shake for a few seconds so that the remaining liquid will evaporate. Pour over about 2 tablespoons of butter and 1 teaspoon of dill and toss.

Finally, serve the pumpkin pie with whipped cream and coffee.

Sweet-Sour Green Beans

This is another of my Aunt Camille's specialties that her guests have raved about for years.

French-cut green beans   two 16-ounce cans, drained
Medium onion   1, cut in rings
Slivered almonds   2-ounce package
Bacon   8 slices
Sugar   ¼ cup
Vinegar   ¼ cup
Salt   ¼ teaspoon
White pepper   ⅛ teaspoon

Layer beans, onion rings, and almonds in 1-quart casserole. Fry the bacon crisp and set aside, reserving drippings. Combine sugar, vinegar, salt, and pepper and pour into bacon drippings. Bring to a boil and pour over beans. Cover and marinate overnight. Meanwhile, crumble bacon and refrigerate it for later use. Do not add to casserole yet. When ready to reheat, sprinkle bacon bits over top of beans and bake uncovered at 350° until bubbly, about 20 to 30 minutes. Serves 6 to 8.

Tropical Brunch for Four

Isthmus Bloody Mary Cocktails*

Deviled Eggs with Caviar

Seafood Crepes Mornay

Chilled Asparagus

Frozen Raspberry Chiffon*

Sweet Leilani Squares*

Chenin Blanc, Sebastiani (California)

Perhaps good friends or your parents are visiting and your task is to entertain them in your home before their departure. This is a most suitable brunch for that occasion. Keep the setting informal, but add color with napkins, placemats, or centerpiece.

Upon their arrival serve Isthmus Bloody Mary Cocktails and the deviled eggs. You may make the Bloody Mary pitcher the day before if you choose, as long as it is well covered. You may also devil the eggs the night before and cover snugly, but wait until just before guests arrive to place a dab of caviar on half of them. On the other half, sprinkle paprika and minced parsley.

You may either cook fresh asparagus or use two cans of good quality spears. Chill well, and when serving, distribute portions on individual plates and top each serving with an X of pimientos and minced egg yolk.

Use Your Basic Crepe Recipe and Create Your Own Crepe together with the recipe for Mornay Sauce (see Index) to make the Seafood Crepes Mornay. Make the crepes the day before and freeze extras; or, if you have some frozen, thaw them. (Remember when freezing them that each crepe must be separated with wax paper.) Allow two crepes per person. You may also make the Mornay Sauce the prior day; place flecks of butter over the top before covering and chilling.

As far as the seafood mixture goes, the sky is the limit. However, a very simple, inexpensive mixture would be sautéed chopped onion, one-half a green bell pepper (diced), and one-fourth pound of sliced mushrooms. Add about one pound of fish fillets chunks for the last minute. Cover and store in refrigerator overnight. When ready to cook, stir in about one-third of the Mornay Sauce and fill crepes. Pour remaining sauce over crepes and bake in a preheated 350° oven for twenty minutes. Serve on individual plates, along with asparagus, and garnish with a clump of parsley and pitted black olives. You may add a slice of ripe tomato if you wish.

The Frozen Raspberry Chiffon may be made in advance also. I often chill this in a lovely crystal bowl and serve individual crystal bowls at the table. However, you may chill it in the individual bowls if you wish. Garnish with mint leaves. Serve with the Sweet Leilani Squares, which may be prepared several days in advance and stored in an airtight container.

Isthmus Bloody Mary

Jim Dittmar, my neighbor and an Isthmus of Catalina Island devotee, makes a terrific Bloody Mary. He serves it at his home on most major holidays and on his sloop at the Isthmus every summer. He makes a pitcher of the Bloody Mary mix in advance and stores it, well covered, in the refrigerator. He does use the large tumblers, also known as buckets. By all means, use a large glass with lots of ice. For those who wish, he rims the edge of the chilled glasses in salt. To rim the glass, rub the edge with lime juice and dip in a saucer filled with coarse salt. However, so many people are salt conscious that he doesn't rim the glass unless they consent.

Undiluted beef bouillon   10½-ounce can
V-8 juice   46-ounce can
Onion powder   1 tablespoon
Garlic powder   1 tablespoon
Coarsely ground pepper   ½ to ¾ teaspoon, depending upon taste
Tabasco   5 drops
Worcestershire sauce   3 tablespoons
Vodka   2 to 3 tablespoons (1 to 1½ shots) per drink, depending upon
  taste
Celery stalks   garnish (optional)

Mix all ingredients together in a pitcher except celery stalks and vodka. Chill well. Pour vodka into individual glasses and fill with Bloody Mary mix. Stir well and garnish with celery stalk if desired. (Rim glasses first

with salt if requested.) Makes 8 large Bloody Mary cocktails.
Variation: Bottled clam juice may be substituted for beef bouillon.

Frozen Raspberry Chiffon

Lemon juice 2 tablespoons
Boiling water ½ cup
Unflavored gelatin 1 tablespoon (1 envelope)
Egg whites 2
Frozen raspberries 10-ounce package, cut in pieces
Mint leaves garnish

Combine lemon juice, boiling water, and unflavored gelatin in blender; cover and run on low for 1 minute or until gelatin dissolves. Add egg whites and frozen raspberry pieces. Cover and run on high until blender feels cool to the touch and chiffon is well mixed. Pour into bowl or individual glasses and chill until firm, at least 3 hours. Garnish with mint leaves. Serves 4.

Sweet Leilani Squares

Flour 1½ cups
Salt 1 teaspoon
Baking soda ½ teaspoon
Butter ½ cup, softened to room temperature
Sugar ½ cup
Eggs 4
Vanilla ¼ teaspoon
Rum extract ¼ teaspoon
Crushed pineapple 13½-ounce can, drained
Nuts (macadamia nuts, pecans, or walnuts) ½ cup chopped
Flaked coconut ½ cup

Grease and line with waxed paper two 9 by 9-inch square pans. Combine flour, salt, and soda and set aside. Cream butter, gradually adding sugar. Blend well. Add one egg at a time, and mix well after each addition. Blend in flour mixture. Stir in vanilla, rum extract, pineapple, nuts, and coconut. Spread in pans and bake at 350° for 30 minutes. Turn out on rack and remove waxed paper. Allow to cool completely before cutting and serving. Makes thirty-six 1½-inch squares or sixteen 2-inch squares.

Hearty Brunch for Six

Enid's Eggs

Kielbasa

Hashbrowns

Pineapple and Strawberries with Vanilla Sauce

Blanc de Blanc, Almadén (California)

This is a superb buffet and one well suited for champagne. The eggs, the kielbasa (which is Polish sausage), and the Vanilla Sauce (see Index) are made the day before. Follow the recipe for Enid's Eggs, and the directions for cooking the kielbasa are in the Fish and Sausage Gumbo recipe.

A basket of fresh strawberries may also be rinsed the day before, and if necessary, you can cut the pineapple the night before, but pour off some of the accumulated juice (drink it!) before you mix with the strawberries. Of course, raspberries (sprinkled with sugar) or other fresh fruits may be substituted, and I suppose, if nothing fresh is available, frozen fruits will do. Fruit served in a glass or crystal bowl gives a refreshing, inviting appearance—elegant, too! Serve the Vanilla Sauce on the side, and do tell your guests what it is for—they will love it!

When getting ready to serve, prepare your favorite (or frozen) hashbrown recipe, make your buttered toast, have hot coffee and tea handy (or champagne if you prefer); and of course, the eggs are steaming and kielbasa hot.

Easy Brunch for Six

Vichyssoise

Celeriac Salad

Shrimp Coquilles with Mousseline Sauce

Watermelon Sherbet

Chessmen Cookies

Verdillac, Armand Roux (France)

This brunch is ideal for the working person because everything is either made in advance and is relatively simple to make, or you can open a can or a carton. Add an elegant setting and your guests will think you slaved for hours.

In summer serve the vichyssoise and watermelon sherbet. If you do not wish to make your own vichyssoise, purchase three cans of Crosse and Blackwell Vichyssoise. Chill them from the moment you take them from the grocery bag. To serve, shake the can, open, and pour into individual soup bowls, sprinkling each with a little chopped parsley or green onion. Hard, isn't it? With my china, one can serves two people. Do remember the parsley or green onion! That adds necessary elegance.

Next serve the Celeriac Salad (see Index) on a bed of lettuce on individual salad plates. Make the salad the day or night before.

Finally serve the entrée, Shrimp Coquilles with Mousseline Sauce, which you have assembled that morning (although you may have cooked the shrimp the previous day). Preheat the broiler and voilà! Done in 4 minutes!

In champagne glasses which you have set out the day before, place a scoop of the sherbet garnished with mint leaves. Serve with Pepperidge Farm's Chessmen Cookies—my favorite!

In winter you may wish to substitute a hot French onion soup for the vichyssoise. Place a crusty slice of fresh French bread in the bottom of each bowl; pour the hot soup over and top with grated Gruyère cheese. In winter, you might substitute the Iced Lemon Tortoni Pie (see Index) for the watermelon sherbet.

Serve this brunch leisurely, dallying between courses, opening another bottle of wine or champagne. A white cloth and flowers or greenery would be lovely.

Bluefish Brunch for Six

Boiled Ham Rolls

Bluefish-Watercress Soufflé

Velouté Sauce

Carottes Vichy*

Kasha

Hot Dinner Rolls

Your Favorite Berry Pie

Brut, Christian Brothers (California)

This is such an easy brunch and equally easy on the budget. You may serve twelve readily by doubling the amounts and making two soufflés. The day before, make the ham rolls, Velouté Sauce, and Carottes Vichy. (For ham rolls, see introduction to Oven-Steamed Kumu with Capers and Wine menu. Since you will be reheating the carrots, cook them only for about fifteen minutes. Make the soufflés either the night before or the morning that you plan to serve them up to the point stated in the recipe where you may refrigerate them.

If you have two regular ovens (microwave will not do), you might substitute Potatoes Anna (see Index) for the kasha, but if you have only one oven, then make the kasha. (Kasha is buckwheat groats and may be found either in the rice or gourmet sections of the market.) Cook according to directions on the box, but allow about ten minutes longer than stated. Use chicken broth or bouillon, not plain water, and add chopped onions and mushrooms when sautéing the kasha. You can even add nuts if you wish, such as chopped filberts or almonds.

The soufflé is lovely on a silver tray with the sauce served in a silver gravy boat; but whatever it is served on, please do garnish.

Carottes Vichy

Fresh baby carrots   12-ounce package
Water   ½ cup
Dark or coarse brown sugar   2 tablespoons
Butter   3 tablespoons
Nutmeg   ⅛ teaspoon
Salt   ¼ teaspoon
Parsley   1 teaspoon minced

Peel and trim baby carrots to 1-inch lengths. (If using regular fresh carrots, slice diagonally into ½-inch widths.) Bring water, brown sugar, butter, nutmeg, and salt to a boil. Boil, stirring constantly, for 1 to 2 minutes until sugar dissolves. Add carrots and cook uncovered on medium-low for 20 minutes, or until just tender. (Cook only 15 minutes if planning to refrigerate, then later reheat for 5 minutes.) Stir occasionally. Drain and toss carrots gently with minced parsley. Serve immediately. Serves 6.

Scandinavian Brunch for Eight

Gravlax

Gravlaxsås

Chilled Poached Eggs

Tiny Boiled Potatoes

Creamed Spinach

Toast

Raspberry Sherbet

Chessmen Cookies

Macon Blanc, Louis Jadot (France)

This buffet is particularly harmonious with an elegant setting and, according to my Swedish friend, should be served with a chilled, dry white wine.
Prepare the Gravlax three days in advance according to the recipe

and slice it ahead of time. Arrange it attractively on a silver tray surrounded by the chilled poached eggs which are made the day before, drained and refrigerated. (Trim the eggs for appearance if necessary.) Arrange clumps of fresh dill or parsley for garnish along with lemon slices. Have a small bowl filled with lemon wedges and another bowl for the Gravlaxsås. In attractive vegetable bowls, serve the hot creamed spinach and the hot boiled potatoes. The toast may rest comfortably on a silver tray.

To make the potatoes, bring salted water to a boil and boil the potatoes for about ten minutes, uncovered. Drain and immediately put back in hot pan. Replace pan over heat and shake the pan for a few seconds so that the remaining liquid may evaporate. Add 3 tablespoons of butter and 1 tablespoon of chervil (or minced parsley) and lightly toss. Serve immediately while hot.

The raspberry sherbet may be served in individual compotes or champagne glasses. My favorite cookies to accompany such light desserts are Pepperidge Farm's Chessmen Butter Cookies.

Casual Brunch for Eight

Deviled Eggs with Caviar

Chilled Cracked Crab

Assorted Sauces

Salade Nicole*

Sourdough French Bread

Harvey Wallbanger Cake with Galliano Orange Sauce*

Your Favorite Beer

In this brunch absolutely everything is made in advance. Begin with the crab. Cook according to the recipe for East Coast Steamed Hard-Shell Crabs, or you may prefer to use the method in Konishi Kona Crab but adding the scallions and red pepper to the water. Allow one-half to one crab per person, depending upon the size of the crabs; for example, a Dungeness crab will usually serve two, in which case you would need four crabs (and you might want to have an extra one for good measure). You can cook the crabs the day before the brunch.

Next cook the potatoes and green beans, cut the sweet red bell pepper, but do not assemble until the morning of the brunch. Also, you can make the sauces the day before. Three sauces would serve nicely; you might try the Blender Aioli Sauce, Curry Mayonnaise, and Watercress Sauce. These would provide interesting variations in taste and appearance. Allow about two cups of each.

You can devil the eggs the night before if you cover them well, but don't put the caviar on until the following morning. On one-half of the eggs, place a dab of caviar and the other half sprinkle with paprika topped with a small piece of chopped parsley.

You can also bake the cake and make the orange sauce the day before, but try to obtain the freshest French bread the day of the brunch if possible. Serve the bread with room temperature butter.

The morning of the brunch assemble the Salade Nicole and crack the crabs. Complete the deviled eggs and arrange them around the platter of cracked crabs. Other garnishes are cucumber slices, tomato slices or cherry tomatoes, olives, and clumps of parsley. A bed of watercress would provide a nice backdrop for the cracked crabs. The sauces should be served in boats or attractive bowls, each with its own spoon. Crack the legs and claws in advance.

On the table arrange the large platter of crabs as the centerpiece. You may wish to arrange identical bowls of sauce on each end of the platter. Arrange the salad, French bread, and butter, and depending upon your serving plans, you might have the plate settings completed, too.

Salade Nicole

Potatoes 8, peeled and sliced
String beans 2 pounds, cut in 1½-inch lengths
Sweet red bell pepper 1, cut in ½-inch squares
Onion 1, minced
Salt to taste
Sauce Vinaigrette (see Index) 1 cup
Parsley garnish
Bacon bits garnish

Cook potatoes and green beans and dry thoroughly. Layer sliced potatoes with green beans, sweet red bell pepper squares, and minced onion. Salt. Drizzle some Sauce Vinaigrette over each layer and repeat. Chill thoroughly. Garnish with chopped parsley and bacon bits. Serves 8.

Harvey Wallbanger Cake

This is another of Jean Hindman's specials. She is particularly fond of cooking with liqueurs, and this is one of her favorites.

Yellow cake mix with pudding   1 package (Be sure pudding is in the mix)
Eggs   4
Vegetable oil   1 cup
Orange juice   ¾ cup
Vodka   ¼ cup
Galliano liqueur   ¼ cup
Galliano Orange Sauce

Mix all ingredients in large mixing bowl and beat with electric mixer at high speed for 4 to 5 minutes. Pour into greased 12-inch bundt pan. Bake in preheated 350° oven for 40 to 45 minutes. Test with toothpick for doneness. Cool and invert cake on serving tray. Sprinkle with powdered sugar and grated orange rind and serve with orange sauce on the side. Serves 10.

Note: If your oven runs hot, bake cake at 325° for 45 minutes.

Galliano Orange Sauce

Sugar   ¼ cup
Cornstarch   2 tablespoons
Water   1 cup
Butter   2 tablespoons
Orange rind   ½ teaspoon grated
Orange juice   2 teaspoons
Galliano liqueur   ½ teaspoon
Vanilla extract   ½ teaspoon

Combine sugar, cornstarch, and water in double boiler and cook over hot water until thickened, stirring constantly. Remove pan from heat. Add remaining ingredients and stir thoroughly. Refrigerate until ready to serve, then warm sauce and serve it on the side. Makes 1 cup.

Chowder Brunch for Ten

Hot Cheese Dip*

Boston Clam Chowder

Buffet Sandwiches

Apple Date Squares*

Your Favorite Beer

Your budget is pinched because Christmas has just passed and you've just learned that your mate has invited a group over to watch the Super Bowl. This brunch may be your solution to providing a delicious, well-rounded meal on a beer budget.

The day before, you may prepare the dip, the chowder, the contents for the buffet sandwiches, and even the Apple Date Squares. Then you may enjoy the game with the rest of the gang.

You may choose from a variety of contents for your sandwiches. Often, I use ham and turkey which I prepare the day prior and cut into squares or one-half sandwich portions. (I freeze what I don't need.) However, other good sandwich possibilities are chicken salad, liverwurst, or assorted cold cuts. Do try to have two offerings so people may choose. If offering liverwurst (which I love!) or cold cuts, provide a few slices of Swiss cheese on the side.

Before your guests arrive, skim the accumulated fat from the chowder as stated in the recipe and refrigerate again until ready to heat. Prepare the sandwich material, such as putting mayonnaise and mustard (Dijon is good) into bowls, alfalfa sprouts into a bowl, and create a plate of sliced tomatoes arranged with individual portions of lettuce leaves. Arrange a small plate of sliced, sweet onions on the side.

Place an assortment of suitable breads in a large glass bowl. For example, if serving ham and turkey, serve party rye with white bread mixed in with a whole wheat variety. For chicken salad and liverwurst, a sliced French bread (if large slices, cut in half) with a whole wheat would be nice.

When your guests arrive, heat the dip and serve with stone ground tortilla chips. Offer your guests beer, soft drinks, or Isthmus Bloody Mary cocktails (see Index).

Hot Cheese Dip

Sharp Cheddar cheese   3 cups grated
Black olives   one and one-half 4½-ounce cans, chopped and drained
Green onions   6, finely chopped
Garlic cloves   2 or 3, pressed, depending upon taste
Canned green chilies   1 tablespoon diced
Mayonnaise   3 tablespoons

Mix all ingredients together and bake at 350° for 20 minutes. (Allow a few minutes longer if refrigerated.) Serve hot with stone ground tortilla chips. Makes 4 cups.

Apple-Date Squares

This is an old family recipe that has been handed down for generations in Jean Hindman's family.

Shortening   ½ cup
Sugar   ¾ cup
Egg   1
Salt   ¼ teaspoon
Baking soda   1 teaspoon
All-purpose flour   1½ cups
Tart apples   2 cups finely chopped
Dates   1 cup chopped
Brown sugar   ¼ cup
Cinnamon   1 teaspoon
Walnuts   ½ cup chopped

Cream shortening and sugar and add egg and beat well. Add salt, baking soda, and flour and beat well. Add apples and dates. Spread into greased oblong baking pan. Mix together brown sugar, cinnamon, and walnuts and sprinkle topping mixture over batter. Bake in preheated 350° oven for 30 to 35 minutes. Makes twenty-four 2-inch squares.

Stamp 'n' Go Luncheon for Four

Stamp 'n' Go Rock Cod Sandwiches

Onion Buns

Fresh Vegetable Medley

Chocolate Cake

Your Favorite Beer

Occasionally there is a need to serve teen-agers who have either shown up or never gone home from your place, and if your mate has just shown up with some kind of rockfish that you've been wanting to do something different with, here is a luncheon that will take care of both.

The large onion buns truly add to the flavor of the whole sandwich, so do seek them out in the bread section of your market.

Make your fresh vegetable salad with anything you have in your refrigerator, but zucchini, cauliflower, and artichoke hearts are a good start. Toss it with an Italian dressing.

Make the sandwiches according to the recipe and be sure to serve with large leaves of crisp lettuce and slices of large tomatoes.

For dessert, a frozen chocolate cake works wonders.

Bridge Luncheon for Eight

Sole with Asparagus and Onion Rings

Green Salad

Lemon Sherbet

Vanilla Wafers

Chablis, Taylor (California)

Many of the luncheons I've attended are related to bridge days. Eight of us will gather for a day of outrageous bidding and amiable play. The hostess, of course, has to spring for the luncheon. Here is an easy one that may be made in advance.

Prepare the sole according to the recipe up to the point indicating the casserole may be refrigerated. Make the green salad (spinach or lettuce) and refrigerate. Time yourself, so that you allow about forty-five minutes to reheat it in an oven or thirty minutes in a microwave, lowering the power in the microwave so the edges don't get overcooked.

Have your sherbet glasses on the counter, ready to be filled—no one wants to wait when playing bridge.

Luncheon Buffet for Eight

Buffet Gateau

Deviled Eggs with Caviar

Chilled Sliced Tomatoes

Crescent Rolls

Parfait Fruit Salad*

Blanc de Blanc, Almadén (California)

Every food in this menu may be prepared in advance, so that you only have to reheat the gateau and bake the crescent rolls. Prepare the gateau according to the directions. The day before, make the fruit salad and pour it into individual parfait glasses and chill. You can also devil the eggs the previous day, but leave the small dollop of caviar until the morning you plan to serve. Also, early that morning you can slice the tomatoes, cover and refrigerate; a little minced parsley sprinkled over the tomatoes adds a nice color. Remember that the gateau is very rich, so cut small wedges; your guests may always return for seconds. A nice accent for the table are assortments of black olives, radishes, and stuffed green olives.

Parfait Fruit Salad

Egg yolks 3, beaten
Sugar 2 tablespoons
Vinegar 2 tablespoons
Pineapple syrup 2 tablespoons
Butter 1 tablespoon
Salt ⅛ teaspoon
Macadamia nuts ½ cup chopped
White cherries 2 cups drained and pitted
Pineapple chunks 2 cups drained
Oranges 2, seeded, peeled, sectioned, and cut in pieces
Miniature marshmallows about 30
Heavy whipping cream 1 cup, whipped
Whipped cream garnish
Mint garnish

Combine egg yolks, sugar, vinegar, pineapple syrup, butter, and salt in a double boiler and stir constantly until thickened. Allow sauce to cool. Stir in nuts, cherries, pineapple chunks, oranges, marshmallows, and 1 cup whipped cream. Fold into parfait glasses and chill for 24 hours. When ready to serve, top with a dollop of whipped cream and a fresh mint sprig. Serves 8 to 10.

U.S. and Metric Measurements

Approximate conversion formulas are given below for commonly used U.S. and metric kitchen measurements.

Teaspoons	×	5	= milliliters
Tablespoons	×	15	= milliliters
Fluid ounces	×	30	= milliliters
Fluid ounces	×	0.03	= liters
Cups	×	240	= milliliters
Cups	×	0.24	= liters
Pints	×	0.47	= liters
Dry pints	×	0.55	= liters
Quarts	×	0.95	= liters
Dry quarts	×	1.1	= liters
Gallons	×	3.8	= liters
Ounces	×	28	= grams
Ounces	×	0.028	= kilograms
Pounds	×	454	= grams
Pounds	×	0.45	= kilograms
Milliliters	×	0.2	= teaspoons
Milliliters	×	0.07	= tablespoons
Milliliters	×	0.034	= fluid ounces
Milliliters	×	0.004	= cups
Liters	×	34	= fluid ounces
Liters	×	4.2	= cups
Liters	×	2.1	= pints
Liters	×	1.82	= dry pints
Liters	×	1.06	= quarts
Liters	×	0.91	= dry quarts
Liters	×	0.26	= gallons
Grams	×	0.035	= ounces
Grams	×	0.002	= pounds
Kilograms	×	35	= ounces
Kilograms	×	2.2	= pounds

Temperature Equivalents

Fahrenheit	− 32	× 5	÷ 9	= Celsius
Celsius	× 9	÷ 5	+ 32	= Fahrenheit

U.S. Equivalents

1 teaspoon	= ⅓ tablespoon
1 tablespoon	= 3 teaspoons
2 tablespoons	= 1 fluid ounce
4 tablespoons	= ¼ cup or 2 ounces
5⅓ tablespoons	= ⅓ cup or 2⅔ ounces
8 tablespoons	= ½ cup or 4 ounces
16 tablespoons	= 1 cup or 8 ounces
⅜ cup	= ¼ cup plus 2 tablespoons
⅝ cup	= ½ cup plus 2 tablespoons
⅞ cup	= ¾ cup plus 2 tablespoons
1 cup	= ½ pint or 8 fluid ounces
2 cups	= 1 pint or 16 fluid ounces
1 liquid quart	= 2 pints or 4 cups
1 liquid gallon	= 4 quarts

Metric Equivalents

1 milliliter	= 0.001 liter
1 liter	= 1000 milliliters
1 milligram	= 0.001 gram
1 gram	= 1000 milligrams
1 kilogram	= 1000 grams

Index

Anchovy paste, 14
Appetizers
  Anchovy Olives, 124
  Buffet Gateau, 110–11
  Caviar and Egg Mousse, 123
  Caviar and Sour Cream Spread, 123
  Caviar Classic, 122
  Caviar over Cream Cheese, 122
  Cherry Tomatoes Stuffed with
    Shrimp, 112
  Christmas Pâté, 119
  Crab Mousse, 120–21
  Crispy Wun Tun, 117
  Curried Shrimp Puffs, 113
  Entrées as, 112
  Fish Lady Fingers, 124
  Hawaiian Fish Balls, 118
  Hawaiian-Style Ceviche, 126
  Hors d'Oeuvre Puff Shells, 113
  Hot Cheese Dip, 188
  Latin American Ceviche, 127
  Lomi Lomi Salmon, 125
  Mousseline (Quenelle) St.
    Jacques, 116
  Poached Oysters in Spinach
    Leaves, 115
  Sashimi, 128
  Savory Clam Puffs, 114
  Shrimp Mousse, 121
  Spinach-Clam Spread, 120
  Sunday Afternoon Lobster, 114–15
  Swordfish Palau Pupu, 124–25

Baked
  Baked Fish with Anchovy Cure, 33
  Baked Fish with Caper Cure, 33
  Baked Fish with Crab Stuffing, 30
  Baked Fish with Florentine Mask, 32
  Baked Fish with Pesto Stuffing, 30–31
  Baked Fish with Shrimp–Bacon
    Stuffing, 29
  Baked Fish with Shrimp–Curry Cure, 32
  Baked Fish with Spinach Stuffing, 28
  Baked Opakapaka with Spinach
    Stuffing, 31
  Baked Squid with Pesto Stuffing, 52–54
  Baked Turbot with Wheat Germ, 43
  Bass Baked in Green Bouillabaisse
    Sauce, 44–45
  Bluefish-Watercress Soufflé, 46–47
  Cajun Fish Rolls, 42–43
  Cheese, Chili, and Shrimp Quiche, 99
  Curried Haddock Casserole, 54
  Enid's Eggs, 38
  Escalloped Oyster Casserole, 41

Green Chili–King Salmon Bake, 51
  Mahimahi–Halibut Supreme, 46
  Mousseline (Quenelle) St. Jacques, 116
  Quiche Saumon, 100
  Seafood Lasagna, 48–50
  Snapper in Mustard and Wine, 42
  Sole with Asparagus and Onion Rings, 44
  Tuna Quesadillas, 98–99
Bamboo shoots, 14
Bamboo skewers, 14
Barbecued
  Barbecued Whole Salmon, 78
  Ono Teriyaki BBQ, 81
  Opakapaka Slow Cook, 80
  Parrot Fish with Sausage, 81
  Polynesian Steelhead BBQ, 83
  Scallops Yakitori, 84–85
Bass
  Bass Baked in Greek Bouillabaisse
    Sauce, 44–45
  Menu, 165–66
  Island Curry, 88–89
  Menu, 147–48
Bean threads, 14
Black Cod
  Black Cod Sukiyaki, 66–67
Bluefish
  Bluefish-Watercress Soufflé, 46–47
  Menu, 182
Boiled
  Konishi Kona Crab, 56
Boning, 66–67
Broiled
  Broiled Halibut with Anchovy Butter, 84
  Broiled Salmon Diable, 79
  Crab with Mousseline Sauce in
    Ramekins, 91
  Curried Shrimp Puffs, 113
  Fresh Maine Lobster with Tarragon
    Butter Sauce, 86
  Grilled Sturgeon with Mushroom
    Sauce, 82
  Savory Clam Puffs, 114
  Shrimp Coquilles with Mousseline
    Sauce, 92

Calamari. See Squid
Capers, 14
Casseroles
  Curried Haddock Casserole, 54
  Escalloped Oyster Casserole, 41
Catfish
  Fried Channel Catfish, 63
Caviar, 122
  Caviar and Egg Mousse, 123

Caviar and Sour Cream Spread, 123
Caviar Classic, 122
  Menu, 173–74
Caviar over Cream Cheese, 122
Celeriac root, 14
Ceviche
  Hawaiian-Style Ceviche, 126
  Latin American Ceviche, 127
  Swordfish Palau Pupu, 124–25
Chinese parsley, 14
Chinese pea pods, 14
Chinese mustard, 14
Chorizo, 14
Chowder
  Boston Clam Chowder, 105
  New England Fish Chowder, 106
  Vegetable Clam Chowder, 107
Chung choi, 15
Clams
  Boston Clam Chowder, 105
    Menu, 187
  Linguine with White Clam Sauce, 93
    Menu, 171
  Savory Clam Puffs, 114
  Spinach-Clam Spread, 120
Cleaning squid, 52–53
Coconut milk, 15
Cod. *See* **Black Cod; Lingcod; Rock Cod**
Combinations. *See also* **Casseroles;**
  Chowder; Gumbo
  Classic Seafood Combo, 36
  St. Charles's Paella for Twenty, 96–97
  Seafood Lasagna, 48–50
Court-Bouillon, 132
Crab
  Basque Scrambled Eggs with Crab, 73
  Crab Mousse, 120–21
  Crab with Mousseline Sauce in
    Ramekins, 91
    Menu, 160
  East Coast Steamed Hard-Shell
    Crabs, 56
  Enid's Eggs, 38
    Menu, 180
  Konishi Kona Crab, 56
Creamed
  Creamed Finnan Haddie, 89
  Creamed Salmon, 90
  Island Curry, 88–89
Crepes
  Basic recipe, 109
  Buffet Gateau, 110–11
  Variations, 110
    Menu, 177–78
Curry. *See* **Bass**
Cuttlefish. *See* **Squid**

Daikon, 15
Dashi-no-moto, 15

Desserts
  Apple-Date Squares, 188
  Baked Pineapple with Custard
    Sauce, 148–49
  Chocolate Chip Cake, 170
  Fresh Nectarine Pie, 159
  Frozen Raspberry Chiffon, 179
  Grandmother Adams's Chocolate
    Sauce, 164–65
  Harvey Wallbanger Cake, 186
  Iced Lemon Tortoni Pie, 175
  Parfait Fruit Salad, 191
  Sorbet de Pamplemousse, 161
  Strawberries Romanoff, 150–51
  Sumptuous Peach Ice Cream, 152
  Sweet Leilani Squares, 179
  Vanilla Sauce, 157
Drinks
  Isthmus Bloody Mary, 178–79

Eel
  Marinated Eel, 75
Entertaining, 144–47
Escoffier Diable Sauce, 15

Finnan Haddie
  Creamed Finnan Haddie, 89
    Menu, 176
Filé Powder, 15
Fish
  Amounts to buy, 13
  Any kind of
    Fish and Sausage Gumbo, 102–3
      Menu, 171-72
    Fish Lady Fingers, 124
    Hawaiian Fish Balls, 118
    Latin American Ceviche, 127
    New England Fish Chowder, 106
    Seafood Lasagna, 48–50
    Uncle Jack's Fish Gumbo, 104
  Boning, 66–67
  Descriptions, 18–25
  Fat content, 9, 10–11, 18–25
  Roe (Caviar), 122–23
  Selecting, 11–13
Fried and sautéed
  Basque Scrambled Eggs with
    Crab, 73
  Black Cod Sukiyaki, 66–67
  Calamari (Fried squid), 94
  Fillets of Sole Meunière, 61
  Fried Channel Catfish, 63
  Fried Trout with Bacon, 58
  Hawaiian Fish Balls, 118
  Island Curry, 88–89
  Lingcod Fish Fry, 71
  Linguine with White Clam Sauce, 93
  Marinated Eel, 75
  Scampi with Fettucine, 90–91

Shark Teriyaki, 65
Shrimp Tempura, 67–69
Snapper à la King for Two, 76
Snapper in Portuguese Vinha D'alhos,
  70–71
Snapper with Pesto Sauce, 62
Sockeye Newburg, 74
Southern Deep-Fried Sauger, 64
Stamp 'n' Go Rock Cod Sandwiches, 72
Sunday Afternoon Lobster, 114–15
Trout Grenobloise, 60
Trout with Almond Paste, 59
Frog legs
Michel's Frog Legs, 60–61

Gravlax. *See* **Salmon**
Gumbo
Fish and Sausage Gumbo, 102–3
Uncle Jack's Fish Gumbo, 104

Haddock
Curried Haddock Casserole, 54
Halibut
Broiled Halibut with Anchovy Butter, 84
Mahimahi-Halibut Supreme, 46
Hawaiian fish
Descriptions, 22–25
Fat content, 22–25

Ito-wakame, 15

Jellied Consommé, 35

Kielbasa, 15
Kombu, 15
Kumu
Oven-Steamed Kumu with Capers and
  Wine, 27–28
Menu, 155–56

Lingcod
Lingcod Fish Fry, 71
Lobster
Fresh Maine Lobster with Tarragon
  Butter Sauce, 86
Menu, 160
Sunday Afternoon Lobster, 114–15

Mahimahi
Classic Seafood Combo, 36
Mahimahi-Halibut Supreme, 46
Menu, 162–63
Mandarin oranges, 15
Marinated. *See* **Ceviche; Gravlax**
Mayonnaise. *See* **Sauces, dressings, and**
  marinades
Mayonnaise cure, 31–33
Measures and equivalents, 192–93

Menus, 147–91
Barbecued Whole Salmon, 169
Bass Baked in Greek Bouillabaisse
  Sauce, 165
Bluefish-Watercress Soufflé, 182
Boston Clam Chowder, 187
Buffet Gateau, 190
Calamari, 172–73
Caviar Classic, 173–74
Chilled Poached Whole Salmon, 173–74
Crab with Mousseline Sauce
  in Ramekins, 160
Creamed Finnan Haddie, 176
Enid's Eggs, 180
Fillets of Sole Meunière, 157–58
Fish and Sausage Gumbo, 171–72
Fresh Maine Lobster with
  Tarragon Butter Sauce, 160
Gravlax, 183–84
Grilled Sturgeon with Mushroom
  Sauce, 153
Island Curry, 147–48
Linguine with White Clam Sauce, 171
Mahimahi-Halibut Supreme, 162–63
Oven-Steamed Kumu with Capers and
  Wine, 155–56
Poached Oysters in Spinach Leaves, 160
Scampi with Fettucine, 167
Seafood Crepes Mornay, 177–78
Shrimp Coquilles with Mousseline
  Sauce, 181
Sole with Asparagus and Onion Rings,
  189–90
Sole with Shrimp Sauce au Gratin, 168
Southern Deep-Fried Sauger, 151–52
Stamp 'n' Go Rock Cod Sandwiches, 189
Trout Grenobloise, 149–50
Mirin, 16
Mullet
Cantonese Steamed Mullet, 39
Steamed Mullet 4-Mile Style, 40
Mussels
Steamed Mussels, 55

Ono
Ono Teriyaki BBQ, 81
Opakapaka
Baked Opakapaka with Spinach
  Stuffing, 31
Opakapaka Slow Cook, 80
Oysters
Escalloped Oyster Casserole, 41
Oven-Steamed Oysters, 55
Poached Oysters in Spinach Leaves, 115

Pacific-Atlantic fish
Descriptions, 18–21
Fat Content, 18–21

Paella
St. Charles's Paella for Twenty, 96–97
Panko, 16
Parrot Fish
Parrot Fish with Sausage, 81
Pickapeppa Sauce, 16
Poached
Chilled Poached Whole Salmon, 35
Classic Seafood Combo, 36
Fish Lady Fingers, 124
Poached Oysters in Spinach Leaves, 115
Poached Salmon with Hollandaise
Sauce, 34
Poached Sole with Bercy Sauce, 40–41
Portuguese Vinha D'alhos, 16

Red Snapper. *See* **Snapper**
Rock Cod
Stamp 'n' Go Rock Cod Sandwiches, 72
Menu, 189
Rock salt, 16
Roe. *See* **Caviar**

Sake, 16
Salads
Fruit and vegetable
Celeriac Salad, 158
Chinese Pea Pod Salad with
Fruit Slices, 163
Cucumbers with Sour Cream, 162
Parfait Fruit Salad, 191
Salade Beatrice, 174–75
Salade Nicole, 185
Tabouleh Salad, 166–67
Seafood
Tuna Niçoise, 98
Salmon
Barbecued Whole Salmon, 78
Menu, 169
Broiled Salmon Diable, 79
Chilled Poached Whole Salmon, 35
Menu, 173–74
Creamed Salmon, 90
Gravlax—Salmon Marinated in Dill,
94–95
Menu, 183–84
Green Chili–King Salmon Bake, 51
Lomi Lomi Salmon, 125
Poached Salmon with Hollandaise
Sauce, 34
Quiche Saumon, 100
Salted salmon, 125
Sockeye Newburg, 74
Sandwiches
Stamp 'n' Go Rock Cod Sandwiches, 72
Menu, 189
Sardines
Christmas Pâté, 119
Sashimi, 128

Sauces, dressings, and marinades
Dessert
Chilled Custard Sauce, 149
Galliano Orange Sauce, 186
Grandmother Adams's Chocolate
Sauce, 164–65
Vanilla Sauce, 157
Salad
Honey Fruit Dressing, 164
Seafood
Beurre Blanc Sauce, 131
Beurre Manié, 130
Blender Aioli Sauce, 142
Butter-Wine Sauce, 139
Cajun Sauce, 134–35
Chilled Asparagus Topping, 51
Chilled Cucumber Sauce, 140
Chilled Watercress Sauce, 140
Chinese Dipping Sauce, 117
Court-Bouillon, 132
Curry Mayonnaise, 139
Gravlaxsås (Mustard and Dill
Sauce), 95
Green Mayonnaise, 140–41
Hot Garlic Butter, 134
Italian Diablo Sauce, 49
Making, 130–31
Mornay Sauce, 138
Mousseline Sauce, 136
Newburg Sauce, 138
Parsley-Garlic Mix, 156
Pesto Sauce, 135
Portuguese Marinade, 70–71
Sauce Vinaigrette, 141
Simple Hollandaise Sauce, 137
Tartar Sauce, 142
Tempura Sauce, 134
Velouté Sauce, 133
Velouté on a Grand Scale, 133
White Sauce, 136–37
Sauger
Southern Deep-Fried Sauger, 64
Menu, 151–52
Sautéed. *See* **Fried and sautéed**
Scallops
Classic Seafood Combo, 36
Mousseline (Quenelle) St. Jacques, 116
Scallops Yakitori, 84–85
Sea Bass. *See* **Bass**
Sesame oil, 16
Shark
Shark Teriyaki, 65
Shrimp
Buffet Gateau, 110–11
Menu, 190
Cheese, Chili, and Shrimp Quiche, 99
Cherry Tomatoes Stuffed with
Shrimp, 112
Classic Seafood Combo, 36

Crispy Wun Tun, 117
Curried Shrimp Puffs, 113
Scampi with Fettucine, 90–91
   Menu, 167
Shrimp Coquilles with Mousseline
   Sauce, 92
   Menu, 181
Shrimp Mousse, 121
Shrimp Tempura, 67–69
Snapper
   Snapper à la King for Two, 76
   Snapper in Mustard and Wine, 42
   Snapper in Portuguese Vinha D'alhos,
   70–71
   Snapper with Pesto Sauce, 62
Sockeye. *See* **Salmon**
Sole
   Cajun Fish Rolls, 42–43
   Fillets of Sole Meunière, 61
   Menu, 157–58
   Poached Sole with Bercy Sauce, 40–41
   Sole with Asparagus and Onion
   Rings, 44
   Menu, 189–90
   Sole with Shrimp Sauce au Gratin, 37
   Menu, 168
Squid
   Baked Squid with Pesto Stuffing, 52–54
   Calamari, 94
   Menu, 172–73
   Cleaning, 52–53
Steamed
   Cantonese Steamed Mullet, 39
   East Coast Steamed Hard-Shell Crabs,
   56
   Oven-Steamed Kumu with Capers
   and Wine, 27–28
   Oven-Steamed Oysters, 55
   Steamed Mussels, 55
Steelhead. *See* **Trout**
Stew. *See* **Casseroles; Chowder;**
Combinations; Gumbo
Stuffings
   Almond Paste, 59
   Crab Stuffing, 30
   Pesto Stuffing, 30–31
   Shrimp-Bacon Stuffing, 29
   Spinach Stuffing, 28
Sturgeon
   Grilled Sturgeon with Mushroom
   Sauce, 82
   Menu, 153
Swordfish
   Classic Seafood Combo, 36
   Hawaiian-Style Ceviche, 126
   Swordfish Palau Pupu, 124–25

Tempura Batter, 69
Teriyaki, 16

Ti leaves, 17
Tofu, 17
Trout
   Fried Trout with Bacon, 58
   Polynesian Steelhead BBQ, 83
   Menu, 161
   Trout Grenobloise, 60
   Menu, 149–50
   Trout with Almond Paste, 59
Tuna
   Tuna Niçoise, 98
   Tuna Quesadillas, 98–99
Turbot
   Baked Turbot with Wheat Germ, 43

Ulua
   Broiled Ulua Pickapeppa Steaks, 85

Vegetables and accompaniments
   Artichoke Bottoms Crowned with
   Sautéed Mushrooms, 175
   Asparagus and Broccoli Vinaigrette, 154
   Baked Cheese Grits, 152
   Carottes Vichy, 183
   Fluffy Mashed Potatoes, 154
   Hostess Potatoes, 170
   Potatoes Anna, 158–59
   Quartered Mushrooms, 156
   Sautéed Green Beans, 150
   Sweet-Sour Green Beans, 176–77

Wasabi, 17
Water chestnuts, 17
Wun tun pi, 17

Notes

Notes

Notes

Notes

Other Cookbooks from Pacific Search Press

The Apple Cookbook by Kyle D. Fulwiler
Asparagus: The Sparrowgrass Cookbook by Autumn Stanley
The Bean Cookbook: Dry Legume Cookery by Norma S. Upson
The Berry Cookbook by Kyle D. Fulwiler
Bone Appétit! Natural Foods for Pets
    by Frances Sheridan Goulart
Canning and Preserving without Sugar by Norma M. MacRae, R.D.
The Carrot Cookbook by Ann Saling
The Crawfish Cookbook by Norma S. Upson
The Dogfish Cookbook by Russ Mohney
The Eggplant Cookbook by Norma S. Upson
Food 101: A Student Guide to Quick and Easy Cooking by Cathy Smith
The Green Tomato Cookbook by Paula Simmons
Mushrooms 'n Bean Sprouts: A First Step for Would-be Vegetarians
    by Norma M. MacRae, R.D.
My Secret Cookbook by Paula Simmons
The Natural Fast Food Cookbook by Gail L. Worstman
The Natural Fruit Cookbook by Gail L. Worstman
Rhubarb Renaissance: A Cookbook by Ann Saling
Roots & Tubers: A Vegetable Cookbook by Kyle D. Fulwiler
The Salmon Cookbook by Jerry Dennon
Starchild & Holahan's Seafood Cookbook by Adam Starchild and James Holahan
Warm & Tasty: The Wood Heat Stove Cookbook by Margaret Byrd Adams
The Whole Grain Bake Book by Gail L. Worstman
Wild Mushroom Recipes by Puget Sound Mycological Society
The Zucchini Cookbook by Paula Simmons